FUNNY, YOU DON'T LOOK LIKE ONE

Observations from a Blue-Eyed Ojibway

FUNNY, YOU DON'T LOOK LIKE ONE

Observations from a Blue-Eyed Ojibway

by Drew Hayden Taylor

Theytus Books Ltd.
Penticton B.C.
Canada

First Edition

THEYTUS BOOKS LTD.
257 Brunswick Street
Penticton, B.C. V2A 5P9

Book Design & Typesetting: Barbara Hager
Cover Design: Aurora Artists
Cover Photo: Thomas King

Special Thanks: Gerry William & Regina (Chick) Gabriel

Printed and bound in Canada

Canadian Cataloguing in Publication Data

Taylor, Drew Hayden, 1962-
Funny, you don't look like one

ISBN 0-919441-64-5

1. Indians of North America--Canada--Humour. I. Title.
PS8589.A885F86 1996   C814'.54   C96-910072-8
PR9199.3.T35F86 1996

The publisher acknowledges the support of the
Canada Council, Department of Canadian Heritage
and the Cultural Services Branch of the Province of
British Columbia in the publication of this book.

CONTENTS

PREFACE

This book is the product of almost five years of putting all my errant thoughts down on paper, on what ever subject, for what ever medium. Sometimes the things I feel are humorous (at least I hope so), other times they are straight forward with a darker edge.

But basically, the contents of this book are simply the ideas and observations of a Native person living in this country we call Canada – the good, the bad and the ugly.

I've travelled all across this country, several times in fact. I've been to easily a hundred reserves or more, even met with Indigenous people from many other parts of this planet, and the one thing I've learned, if nothing else, is that there is always a story hiding somewhere – behind a bush, in the next cup of tea, or perhaps the next person who walks in through that door. The real talent in life is being able to know this simple fact, and to look for those stories.

The articles and essays within this book have many homes and many origins. I would like to thank the following media organizations for their support, interest and non-bouncing cheques: *This Magazine, Windspeaker, CBC Radio, Kahtou, The Globe & Mail, Anishinabek News, The Toronto Star,* and the whole damn world!

Drew Hayden Taylor

In this big, huge world, with all its billions and billions of people, it's safe to say that everybody will eventually come across personalities and individuals who will touch them in some peculiar yet poignant way. Individuals that in some way represent and help define who you are. I'm no different – mine is Kermit the Frog. Not just because Natives have a long tradition of savouring frogs legs, but because of his music. You all may remember Kermit is quite famous for his rendition of *It's Not Easy Being Green*. I can relate. If I could sing, my song would be *It's Not Easy Having Blue Eyes in a Brown Eyed Village*.

Yes, I'm afraid it's true. The author happens to be a card carrying Indian. Once you get past the afore-mentioned eyes, the fair skin, light brown hair, and noticeable lack of cheek bones, there lies the heart and spirit of an Ojibway storyteller. Honest 'Injun' or as the more politically correct term may be 'Honest Aboriginal.'

You see, I'm the product of a White father I never knew, and an Ojibway woman who evidently couldn't run fast enough. As a kid I knew I looked a bit different but, then again, all kids are paranoid when it comes to their peers. I had a fairly happy childhood, frolicking through the bulrushes. But there were certain things that even then made me notice my unusual appearance. Whenever we played cowboys and Indians, guess who had to be the bad guy (the cowboy)?

It wasn't until I left the reserve for the big bad city, that I became more aware of the role people expected me to play, and the fact that physically I didn't fit in. Everybody seemed to have this preconceived idea of how every Indian looked and acted. One guy, on my first day of college, asked me what kind of horse I preferred. I didn't have the heart to tell him 'hobby.'

I've often tried to be philosophical about the whole thing. I have both White and Red blood in me. I guess that makes me pink. I am a 'Pink Man.' Try to imagine this: I'm walking around on any typical reserve in Canada, my head held high, proudly announcing to everyone, "I am a Pink Man." It's a good thing I ran track in school.

My pinkness is constantly being pointed out to me over and over and over again. "You don't look Indian?" "You're not Indian, are you?" "Really?!?!" I got questions like that from both White and Native people. For a while I debated having my Status card tattooed on my forehead.

And like most insecure people and especially a blue-eyed Native writer, I went through a particularly severe identity crisis at one point. In fact, I admit it, one depressing spring evening I died my hair black. Pitch black.

The reason for such a dramatic act, you ask? Show business. You see, for the last eight years or so, I've worked in various capacities in the performing arts, and as a result I often get calls to be an extra or even try out for an important role in some Native-oriented movie. This anonymous voice would phone, having been given my number, and ask if I would be interested in trying out for a movie. Being a naturally ambitious, curious and greedy young man, I would always readily agree, stardom flashing in my eyes and hunger pains from my wallet.

A few days later I would show up for the audition, and that was always an experience. What kind of experience you ask? Picture this: the movie calls for the casting of 17th century Mohawk warriors living in a traditional longhouse. The casting director calls the name Drew Hayden Taylor, and I enter. The casting director, the producer, and the film's director look up and see my face, blue eyes flashing in anticipation. I once was described as a slightly chubby beach boy. But even beach boys have tans. Anyway, there would be a quick flush of confusion, a recheck of the papers, a hesitant "Mr. Taylor?" Then they would ask if I was at the right audition. It was always the same. By the way, I never got any of the parts I tried for, except for a few anonymous crowd shots. Politics tells me it's because of the way I look, reality tells me it's probably because I can't act. I'm not sure which is better.

It's not just film people either. Recently I've become quite involved in theatre – Native theatre to be exact. And one cold October day I was happily attending the Toronto leg of a province-wide tour of my first play, *Toronto at Dreamers Rock*. The place was sold out, the audience very receptive, and the performance was wonderful. Ironically one of the actors was also half-White. The director later told me he had been talking with that actor's father, an older non-Native chap. Evidently he had asked a few questions about me, and how I did my research. This made the director curious and asked about his interest. He replied, "He's got an amazing grasp of the Native situation for a white person."

Not all these incidents are work-related either. One time a friend and I were coming out of a rather up-scale bar (we were out Yuppie watching) and managed to catch a cab. We thanked the cab driver for being so comfortably close on such a cold night, he shrugged and nonchalantly talked about knowing what bars to drive around. "If you're not careful, all you'll get is drunk Indians." I hiccuped.

Another time, the cab driver droned on and on about the government. He started out by criticizing Mulroney, and eventually to his handling of the Oka crisis. This perked up my ears, until he said, "If it were me, I'd have tear-gassed the place by the second day. No more problems." He got a dime tip. A few incidents like this and I'm convinced I'd make a great undercover agent for Native political organizations.

But then again, even Native people have been known to look at me with a fair amount of suspicion. Many years ago when I was a young man, I was working on a documentary on Native culture up in the wilds of Northern Ontario. We were at an isolated cabin filming a trapper woman and her kids. This one particular 9-year-old girl seemed to take a shine to me. She followed me around for two days both annoying me and endearing herself to me. But she absolutely refused to believe that I was Indian. The whole film crew tried to tell her but to no avail. She was certain I was White. Then one day as I was loading up the car with film equipment, she asked me if I wanted some tea. Being in a hurry I declined the tea. She immediately smiled with victory, crying out, "See, you're not Indian. All Indians drink tea!"

Frustrated and a little hurt I whipped out my Status card and showed it to her. Now there I was, standing in a Northern Ontario winter, showing my Status card to a 9-year-old non-status Indian girl who had no idea what one was. Looking back, this may not have been one of my brighter moves.

But I must admit, it was a Native woman that boiled everything down in one simple sentence. You may know that woman – Marianne Jones from *The Beachcombers* television series. We were working on a film together out west and we got to gossiping. Eventually we got around to talking about our respected villages. Her village is on the Queen Charlotte Islands, or Haida Gwaii as the Haida call them, and mine is in central Ontario.

Eventually, childhood on the reserve was being discussed and I made a comment about the way I look. She studied me for a moment, smiled and said, "Do you know what the old women in my village would call you?" Hesitant but curious, I shook my head. "They'd say you were pretty like a white boy." To this day I'm still not sure if I like that.

Now some may argue that I am simply a Metis with a Status card. I disagree – I failed French in grade 11. And the Metis, as everyone knows, have their own separate and honourable culture, particularly in western Canada. And, of course, I am well aware that I am not the only person with my physical characteristics.

I remember once looking at a video tape of a drum group, shot on a reserve up near Manitoulin Island. I noticed one of the drummers seemed quite fair-haired, almost blond. I mentioned this to my girlfriend of the time and she shrugged saying "Well, that's to be expected. The highway runs right through the reserve." Perhaps I'm being too critical. There's a lot to be said for both cultures. For example, on the one hand, you have the Native respect for Elders. They understand the concept of wisdom and insight coming with age.

On the White hand, there's Italian food. I mean I really love my mother and family but seriously, does anything really beat good Veal Scaloppine? Most of my Aboriginal friends share my fondness for this particular type of food. Wasn't there a warrior at Oka named Lasagna? I found it ironic, though curiously logical, that Columbus was Italian. A connection I wonder?

Also, Native people have this wonderful respect and love for the land. They believe they are part of it, a mere link in the cycle of existence. Now as many of you know, this conflicts with the accepted Judeo-Christian i.e. western view of land management. I even believe somewhere in the first chapters of the Bible it says something about God giving man dominion over nature. Check it out, Genesis 4 (?): Thou shalt clear cut. So I grew up understanding that everything around me is important and alive. My Native heritage gave me that.

And again, on the White hand, there's breast implants. Darn clever them White people. That's something Indians would never have invented, seriously. We're not ambitious enough. We just take what the Creator decides to give us, but no, not the White man. Just imagine it, some serious looking White (and let's face it people, we know it was a man who invented them) doctor sitting around in his laboratory muttering to himself, "Big tits, big tits, hmm, how do I make big tits?" If it was an Indian, it would be, "Big tits, big tits, White women sure got big tits," and leave it at that.

So where does that leave me on the big philosophical score board? What exactly are my choices again? Indians – respect for Elders, love of the land. White people – food and big tits. In order to live in both cultures I guess I'd have to find an Indian woman with big tits who lives with her grandmother in a cabin out in the woods and can make Fettuccini Alfredo on a wood stove.

Now let me make myself clear – I'm not writing this for sympathy, or out of anger, or even some need for self-glorification. I am just setting the facts straight. For as you read this, a new Nation is born. This is a declaration of independence. My declaration of independence.

I've spent too many years explaining who and what I am repeatedly, so as of this moment, I officially secede from both races. I plan to start my own separate nation. Because I am half Ojibway, and half Caucasian, we will be called the Occasions. And of course, since I'm founding the new nation, I will be a Special Occasion.

1
WHY THE NATIVES ARE RESTLESS

AN OJIBWAY IN MOHAWK TERRITORY

Technically I'm only a few hours, perhaps no more than half a dozen, from home, an Ojibway community tucked away in south central Ontario. But here I sit in a Mohawk community just across the bridge from Montreal, and I feel quite far away from where I learned about life.

Oh there are many things similar to what I'm used to. Not more than two hours ago I had a hearty bowl of macaroni soup, something I've had the pleasure of growing up with and then sampling in Native homes all across the country. In fact, a friend and I are responsible for introducing this delicacy to the Maori, the Aboriginal people of New Zealand as a 'typical Canadian Aboriginal meal.' One chap over there even had three helpings to honour us. I think it's definitely some sort of Indigenous thing, macaroni soup is.

Other things of familiarity remind me of home. The fact that practically everybody is related in some sort of way, the importance of hockey in everyday childhood life. These are Mohawk communities that speak English – a constant irritation to the Quebec government. But for the profusion of Mohawk and American accents that abound here, I feel quite at home. Yet every time somebody asks me if I speak my own language, Ojibway, I automatically respond with a straight face, "Un petit peu." I think the Mohawks are beginning to doubt my allegiances.

But there is a different feel here from the one I grew up with on the reserve or now know in Toronto. One that gnaws at me because I am unfamiliar with it. People around here tell me it existed before the pivotal summer of 1990, the summer of discontent, but intensified during and soon after.

I am talking about the anger, and in some cases, open hatred that exists in this small community. I am well aware that the majority of Native communities in Canada are all angry about something: at the government (Federal, Provincial, Municipal, even their own Aboriginal), at various industries, authorities, individuals, or even just White people in general. Why not, they make up most of the people in the other categories.

But I've never seen this quiet rage so focused as here. Especially among the youth. In my scant 10 days amidst these future leaders of the Mohawk Nation, I've asked several youth what three main things they had on their minds, or if they had the power, what would they change about their lives.

The number one answer: the Surete Du Quebec. Almost every teenager I met told of some harassment by the SQ, before and since the fireworks of the 1990 summer.

In one community, they are almost no longer called the SQ. Local nicknames run towards the always popular and universal *Kwis-Kwis*, 'pig' for all those not fluent in the Mohawk language.

One would tend to chalk it all up to a certain amount of paranoia on their part except for the fact that while I happened to be there, the SQ pumped 15 bullets in a car driven by Mohawks, forcing it off the road. This happened just a few miles from where I was visiting. Fifteen bullets are enough to make anybody wonder.

Warrior checkpoints are still up in some places, anticipating an eventual attack by the above-mentioned SQ. And there is always talk of undercover SQ and RCMP coming in, supposedly to buy cigarettes, but actually to "case the community."

While exploring the grounds surrounding a local survival school, one teacher glanced outside her classroom and noticed me walking against the cold fall wind. Her students immediately turned their heads, one by one like a domino effect, to peer at me. Her immediate reaction was to phone the school office to report "a strange man walking around the property" and to find out my identity.

A safe enough practice at any school perhaps but I got the feeling it wasn't just perverts they were looking out for.

But perhaps the most telling evidence of the political climate these kids are growing up in happened at a school Halloween party. As often happens this time of the year, the school was holding a costume contest. A large portion of the students and teachers showed up in costumes and paraded around the cafeteria while being judged for prizes.

There was the usual variety of costumes, various witches, horror movie characters, tramps and historical figures. There was the teacher that dressed up as Brian Mulroney complete with rumpled suit and a chin down to his navel. And then there was the student who came as the Mohawk Warrior, all in camouflage, including the handkerchief to hide his face. As they paraded and pranced around the cafeteria, the student pulled out his plastic gun and held it to Mulroney's head, threatening him. Teachers and students laughed and cheered, even urged him on. Then he pointed the gun at another teacher dressed in a gorilla suit with the Quebec flag tied around him like a cape. The crowd responded even louder.

But I think I can safely say they didn't cheer out of homicidal anger or a predilection to violence as some would believe. I've known too many Mohawks in my life to even consider this as an explanation. In fact, a family in each of the two communities that I had visited opened their homes and hearts to me, a total stranger, and welcomed me. The families were more than willing to share with and welcome those who were also willing to reciprocate. The Mohawks don't believe the SQ nor the government want to.

When I first arrived in these communities, I wondered what kind of effect living under these conditions would have on these school kids: the tension, the anger, the constant threat of attack. But I should have been worried more about myself. Because in the 10 days I have been here, feeling both the warmth of the people and the animosity between Province, country and community, I have unknowingly been affected. Back in the cafeteria, I was cheering for the warrior. I wasn't even from these people, but I had caught the fever.

SUMMER OF OUR DISCONTENT REVISITED

It seems that opinions about the treatment of the all-too-frequent Native crisis are being voiced more openly. Or more accurately, there appears to be a double standard in relation to blockades: a belief that perhaps Natives are getting preferential treatment, and getting handled with kid gloves.

Tell that to Dudley George, the Ojibway man killed at Ipperwash.

Many critics outside and within the government have commented that there seems to be two sets of laws in Canada: one for the Native people and one for Whites. As I've often heard said, "You get White people blockading a road or doing what the Indians are doing and the police would be in there breaking things up faster than Mike Harris can hit a golf ball. They should treat them Indians like they would White people."

Equal rights – what a concept. That would be nice. Very nice in fact, but in reality, unlikely. It does seem there is a double standard. Chief Tom Bressette of the Stony-Kettle Reserve agrees with these irate voices, basically saying there are "two separate laws" for Indians and Whites, and that Indians "get the lower end of the stick."

Anyone who is even slightly familiar with the Native community is well aware of the incredibly high levels of Aboriginal people incarcerated in the Provincial and Federal jails. While Native people make up less than five percent of the general population, they sometimes exceed forty percent of those in jail.

You don't have to work for Revenue Canada to know that something is wrong with these numbers. Especially when you take into consideration Native culture, as a whole, never had

jails nor really a need for them. There was no institutional-
ized punishment, no witness relocation, no prison riots.

To go from a culture with no use for jails, to an obscenely
high incarceration rate should tell these politicians and nay
sayers something is dreadfully wrong. Either, in a scant few
years, we as people have become an anarchic gang of hood-
lums with no appreciation of law or government, bent on over-
crowding prisons for the hell of it, or there *is* a double standard. The justice system's famous inflexibility or inability to
take into account different perceptions of what is right and
what is wrong is legendary. For instance, White society
reveres the nuclear family principle, while the Native community is structured around the extended family concept.
Such misunderstanding led to incidents like 'the scoop up'
when thousands of Native kids were forcibly removed from
communities and put up for adoptions, and moved into residential schools.

Centuries of alienation, dispossession, and insensitivity
have also had their effect. When you take away from Native
people their culture, their language, and their land, it creates
a vacuum. And as White scientists love to quote, nature hates
a vacuum.

Logically, something has to fill this gaping black hole.
Anger and frustration at what has been lost or taken rushes
into that vacuum. Simple physics. And while I and the vast
majority of Native people across this country do not condone
violence, I challenge any people with this history not to be
overcome by emotions such as these.

Hugh MacLennan was incredibly naive when he wrote his
book *Two Solitudes*. He couldn't even begin to understand how
many solitudes there really are.

THE TWO NEW SOLITUDES

When I was going to college in Toronto, about 12 years and 15 pounds ago, I met this girl. She was about my age and spoke with the most darling French Canadian accent. Having grown up on a Native reserve, this was my first time in the city and I was anxious to make friends. Especially pretty ones.

So as the days passed we spent time hanging around together, developing a friendship, and teasing each other the way only teenagers can. At one point, after some disagreement I've since long forgotten, she laughed and punched my arm saying "All you English are alike." I distinctly remembered looking around my immediate area trying to figure out who she was talking about. Puzzled, I looked at her saying "I'm not English. I'm Native."

She hummed and hawed, somewhat embarrassed, trying to save her position. "Well I meant all you English-speaking people are alike."

Unfortunately she was right in one respect – English was my first language, not Ojibway like it should be, but that was not the relevant point here. So, trying to appear as philosophical as possible, I countered with, "So does that mean I can say all you White people are alike, English and French? That's the same?" She shook her head saying "That's different."

That was a long time ago. Or so it seemed. Looking back on this snippet of my life, I can't help but think how prophetic this was considering the situation that now exists in Quebec. Evidently it is still 'different.'

I recently returned from spending three weeks in wonderful

downtown Montreal. A remarkably civilized city where you can get a fine bottle of wine at the local store and it has, I believe, the highest per capita of quality restaurants in Canada. It also has, unfortunately, a strong and growing dislike of its Aboriginal people.

And it's this I don't understand because it defies logic. One would think they would be natural allies, both parties being formally oppressed by the Federal Government throughout history. But, as has happened so many times throughout the ages, the oppressed have become the oppressor. Now Native people in that province find themselves threatened at practically every corner, from the Cree who might find themselves doing the back stroke in mercury-contaminated water due to the James Bay Project, to the Mohawk's understandable wariness of Oka cheese and golf.

I couldn't help but notice during my stay in Montreal that in several of the newspapers it was free reign on Mohawk bashing by one or more of the local columnists. It would seem on the surface the Mohawks are the single biggest threat to the people of Quebec since Mordecai Richler's *Oh Canada, Oh Quebec.*

The funny thing is, I know these Mohawk people. They are no threat or at least they don't want to be a threat. Most of them would love the chance to live in domestic harmony with their neighbours, attend Euchre tournaments together, play bingo, all that sort of stuff. It's no fun living your life like a veal lover in a vegetarian store.

But like any typical Native person in this country, I shouldn't be surprised at blatant racism. As it was once said, "Racism is as Canadian as hockey." Well, in some cases, both require big sticks.

Though it's been my experience that the racism in Quebec is quite different from the kind that predominates out west. In the western Provinces, the racism consists of Native people supposedly not living up to the lifestyle enjoyed and embraced by the dominate culture. Case in point, "Indians are lazy, always on welfare, bums, drunks, etc." The dislike stems from the perception of Native people being weaker and more dysfunctional.

In Quebec, however, the racism is based on a completely different level. The Native people are perceived as being equals, and more importantly, and therefore more dangerously, that equality is perceived as being a threat to the sovereignty of the Quebec people. The Native people want, or in some cases claim, the same thing the French want – self government. And evidently you cannot have two race cars on the same track. They will bump into each other too often.

It's been said that in good relationships, the similarities overcome the differences, and it's those differences that make the relationship exciting. Maybe, but it wasn't long before my French Canadian friend and I stopped seeing each other. And a relationship can't get much more exciting than the incidents at Oka.

So I guess after all's said and done (and there's a lot that's been said and done), there are still no answers. Not even questions. Welcome to Canada.

ICH BIN EIN OJIBWAY

The phone call came on a lazy Thursday afternoon which wasn't that unusual since those are the only type of Thursday afternoons I practice. The voice on the other end was from some sort of international institute for Canadian studies and she wanted to know what I was doing the following Thursday. I checked my anemic calender and replied "Nothing. Why?"

"Would you like to come to Germany for eight days?" Quickly my mind raced over everything I had heard about Germany – beer, schnapps, frauleins and something I'd vaguely heard about some wall coming down. That was enough for me and it wasn't long before I was hunting down my underused passport and practicing my "Ich bin ein Ojibway."

It seems there was going to be a conference at some university in Marburg, Germany about 'Canada's Indigenous People,' and I guess they wanted a real live one to attend. It seems their first choices, Daniel David Moses and Maria Campbell for one reason or another, couldn't make it, so I was third on the list (always the bridesmaid, never the bride).

I should have known it was going to be a strange trip right from the beginning. There I was, waiting to board my plane at Pearson Airport when I happened to glance in the duty free shop. There, piled high, calling to my Aboriginal background, was a display advertising 'A Traditional Native Canadian Meal.' I could feel the heart beat of countless generations beating in my chest as I read what was contained in the genuine wood box: Indian bannock, wilderness tea (apple/cranberry), smoked trout, wild rice. It was enough to inspire me to send a care package home. My poor mother doesn't drink nearly enough apple/cranberry wilderness tea let alone bread all the way from India.

Once on the plane I ended up having what at first started out to be a pleasant conversation with a teenager on his way to Israel by way of Germany. His parents had bought him a new CD walkman and he was proudly showing it off. His parents had also thoughtfully provided him with some CD's to listen to on the way there, until he had the chance to buy his own in Israel. At one point during the seven hour flight, he asked me if I wanted to listen to his walkman. I innocently asked what kind of music he had that I could listen to. He then rummaged around in his bag and brought out a new CD with the plastic still on it.

"This one is Ray Charles. You look old. You should like him." It was a longer flight then I had expected but thoughts of stuffing him, his walkman, and Ray Charles in the overhead luggage bin made me pass the time merrily.

Germany itself was a wonderful time, once I got over the porno shop in the airport lobby, and seeing people walk around happily stuffing their faces with french fries covered in mayonnaise – both of which I neglected to experience. My tastes are a little too conservative in both areas.

But soon it was time to pay my bill, so to speak. I was immediately whisked away to the conference in Marburg, a cute and adorable hamlet somewhere in the north-western part of the country. I was asked to sit in on the almost two dozen lectures being given on Native people. They ranged from topics as diverse as 'The Subversive Humour in Maria Campbell's *Halfbreed*,' to 'Feminism in Canadian First Nation's Poetry' to the always exciting 'Selected Problems of the Canadian Micmac.'

I say always exciting sarcastically because most of the lectures were given in German. I felt like I was trapped in a continuous rerun of *Das Boot*. One of the students was provided as an adhoc interpreter but having somebody whisper in your ears for two and a half days can give you a headache. I never did learn how to say, "Do you have any aspirin?" in German.

But by far the high point of the conference was a particu-lar paper given (luckily in English) called 'Environmental Conflicts: Hydro-projects at James Bay.' Basically it was about the Cree's successful efforts to cancel the electrical contract between Hydro-Quebec and New York State.

After delivering her paper (quite well I might add), she opened the floor up for discussion of the work. Immediately a man off to the left of the room put up his hand and instantly proceeded to point out little inaccuracies in her paper and crit-icized her method of research.

Someone whispered into my ear that this gentleman was a representative of the Quebec government, stationed in Germany, sort of like the equivalent of a Provincial Ambassador. The man then started to talk about how, unlike any of the other Provinces, Quebec is quite proud of the rela-tionship and dialogue it has set up with its Aboriginal people, and the unique bond they have forged together!

I began thinking – is this the same Quebec that is in Canada? The same one containing the community known as Kanehsatake, often incorrectly referred to as Oka? What about Restigouche? Feeling that I had to say something or turn in my Status card, I brought that up for discussion. No sooner had I sat down then a woman behind me stood up and said that I, in an obvious French accent "Shouldn't bring Oka into this – half the people there weren't even Canadians."

I debated going into the whole concept of the Iroquois Confederacy not recognizing the border but I noticed the poor presenter standing at the front of the room. Evidently the dis-cussion planned for her paper was going slightly off topic so I decided not to pursue the subject. I still occasionally bleed from where I bit my lip.

The rest of the trip was fantastic and incredible. People were wonderful, beer tasty, and there were sausages galore. It was interesting seeing buildings that were older than when what's-his-name stumbled on Turtle Island (there went the neighbourhood).

But I had an interesting thought as I stood there, looking around at what is often called the Old World. If what's-his-name could 'discover' a continent with an estimated 100 million people already living there, why couldn't I?

Unfortunately the Dusseldorf authorities don't take kindly to flags being planted in their city square. So much for the short term rise and fall of the empire of Drewland.

PARADISE LOST

Well it's finally happened. You can only keep a secret for so long. Especially one as big as this one. And leave it to a Reform Party MP to let the cat out of the bag. Yes, I'm afraid what you've heard is true. The entire Native population of Canada has been living under a veil of untruth.

Last month, Reform MP Herb Grubel compared the Native people of this country to children living on a South Seas Island, financially supported by an over anxious rich uncle – like the Federal Government. Well you could hear the Aboriginal gasp echo from reserves all across this country called Canada.

To put it bluntly, our secret is out. The last five hundred years of oppression, genocide, brainwashing, disease and other assorted afflictions were all a vast and incredibly well managed smoke screen. The truth is it was all an ingenious master plan to achieve this wonderfully luxurious and envied position we now relish.

The fact that we enjoy a suicide rate five times the national average, the knowledge that most Native communities sit at the bottom of the economic ladder and in some cases suffer from grinding poverty, are just a few well established facts that have been exposed for the false rumours and illusions they are.

As the perceptive Mr. Grubel insinuated, the reality is that our existence is actually quite similar to life in the South Sea Islands. I have been to the South Pacific, as I'm sure Mr. Grubel has, or he no doubt wouldn't have made such a comparison.

I, like him, couldn't help but notice the similarities. For

instance, an amazing loss of Indigenous tongues to the all powerful English language, bitterly increased rates of alcoholism, annoying paternal attitudes by colonial governments, and worst of all, hordes and hordes of pesky sunburnt tourists. And as Mr. Grubel no doubt picked up on, we Indigenous people share many of the same cultural habits that we developed as we whiled away the hours on our sun drenched beaches. It's a little known fact that the Maori of New Zealand once occupied a golf course that was illegally built on ancestral land. Sound familiar? Mohawks. Maori. They all look alike.

And I guess when it comes to the South Pacific/North America connection, the biggest shock to people is the news that every night, when it's daytime in the South Pacific, the Queen Charlotte Islands detach and are moved to the South Pacific where Haida people become Polynesians. I'm sure Mr. Grubel has seen these people, sitting on the beaches, in their sweetgrass skirts, carving totem poles out of coconut trees. I hear Gilligan was half Salish.

So as the warm tropical breezes start to blow across my designer buckskin shorts – paid for by the overly generous Federal Government, I must bid you adieu. The luau/bingo is about to begin.

WHY THE BUTT STOPS HERE

No doubt Canada has now reached almost mythic proportions around the world for the way it can take simple little incidents involving Native people and try their darndest to blow them so far out of proportion that the eye can't even focus on them. If not for the want and greed of a nine hole golf course, who would have ever heard of that small town called Oka?

And who would have ever thought a simple package of cigarettes would have been the first substantial stumbling block of the new Liberal Government, not to mention the first significant tax cut this country has seen in a long time? Only in Canada you say? Incredible.

Follow the news and you'll see what I mean. What's happening in Europe? More reports from the battle-plagued arena known as Bosnia-Herzogovina. In the United States, more bad movie plots surface in the Harding-Kerrigan spectacle in an admittedly over reported assault case. And in Canada, it was cigarette smuggling and Mohawks.

I suppose we should be quite delighted that we as a nation don't have nearly the problems the other two have but still, the lunacy of the subject matter makes it hard to be proud. Smoking can be hazardous to the health of the party of power. Especially considering that when you examine the issue, the Mohawks case for their right to sell these well-publicized cigarettes is valid. Though it may be now a moot pointy, the principle is still there. Just examine the justification.

1. What happens on Mohawk land is Mohawk business. The Mohawks say they are a sovereign nation not subject to the laws of Canada or the United States. And they evidently have the paperwork to prove it too, including a number of

wampums and signed treaties. Yeah, like those have ever been honoured! You have to give these people and all Native peoples a round of applause for their unwavering belief that somebody somewhere will actually live up to these agreements. And someday government will balance the budget too.

2. The growing reluctance of all Native people to allow non-Native people to keep telling them what they can and can't do. Everybody remembers what happened last time. We all went to bed and woke up the next morning living on reserves, speaking a foreign language, and practicing a new religion. Borrowing a phrase from another greatly oppressed minority – "Never again! Never again!"

3. They have to make money somehow. It's a well-known fact that many Native communities suffer from a very low level of economic growth. Partly because banks are unwilling to lend money for business projects because technically individuals on the reserve don't 'own' their land. It is held in trust for us by the government and therefore we don't have the collateral necessary to borrow and participate in the economic prosperity that is Canada. Give us the right to go into debt like the rest of the country.

4. Alanis Obomsawin needs a new film to produce. How else can you follow up the success of her *Kanehsatake: 270 Years of Resistance.*' I wonder if she smokes?

5. Mohawks, like the rest of Canada's Native people, don't recognize the imaginary dotted line that separates the Maple Leaf from the Stars and Stripes. The whole philosophy of this piece of land being different from that piece of land is a very bizarre concept. This could only come from the same people who invented Coach, Business, and First Class for the same vehicle.

6. Mohawks are not going to continue to pay cigarette taxes to support the government's pet projects like the James Bay 2 Hydroelectric project which will flood out thousands of their Cree brothers, or pay the salaries of the SQ who have such a charmed relationship with Quebec's Aboriginal people,

or help fund the low level flying up in the Province's north-east corner that is disrupting the Innu's livelihood.

7. It's tradition. Didn't Native people introduce tobacco to the White man? There were no taxes back then. And like always, this tradition has been taken away and appropriated. I think they're turning into Caucasian-givers.

8. What else are the Mohawk going to do? They could operate a bingo palace, but then again they'd have to apply for a gaming license from the Provincial government and that wouldn't be kosher for a sovereign nation. Then the police would come in and, well we've seen that all before. They could reap the benefits of the land and become fishermen. Nope, they couldn't do that after what happened at Restigouche back in '81 when the SQ stormed the place, arresting indiscriminately and confiscating salmon nets they claimed were illegal. Geez, their damned if they do, and damned if they don't.

9. The CBC needs new incidents in everyday Native life to dramatize. How about *Conspiracy of Cigarettes?* How about a television series starring two undercover RCMP officers investigating the illegal smuggling of cigarettes across the Canada/U.S. border. It could be called *Akwesasne Vice.*

10. And perhaps the best reason. It pisses Sheila Copps off. It's so much fun to watch her get angry.

THE FISH/INDIAN WARS

Okay, I'm confused. Maybe somebody out there can explain it to me. Canada, the great country that it is, gets very upset when Spanish trawlers invade what Canada considers to be 'their territory' to fish for some fish nobody had ever heard of called a turbot.

So as self-proclaimed 'Custodians of the Fish Stock,' and to save the fishing industry in Eastern Canada, they must open fire on these fishing boats to make their point.

Okay, I accept that. Admittedly I know practically nothing about foreign affairs and if Ottawa says it's important, I'm willing to believe. I've got nothing against the turbot. Never met one but I'm sure they're a fine fish. Fish Power!!! Maritime power!!!

But a few weeks later, the government turns around and triples the number of low level military flights over the Innu hunting lands. You remember the Innu, the Aboriginal people of Labrador that have been fighting the unwarranted invasion of their traditional homeland by incredibly thunderous fighter jets.

It seems the loud and sudden noises not only scare the you-know-what out of the Innu but also the caribou and other animals they hunt.

Now let's recap. Ottawa is willing to practically go to war over Spanish over-fishing, to preserve a way of life for Canadian fishermen. Ottawa is also willing to ignore its own increased and unwanted presence roaring over Innu land that will, quite probably, end a way of life that has existed for thousands of years.

Now what's wrong with this picture. The fish are worth

protecting but the Innu aren't. Hmmmm?

One suggestion to rectify the situation is to have the Innu change their name to Turbot, and vice versa. That way, their culture will be preserved, if only a little oddly named, and the low level jets can have a heck of a time scaring the hell out of the Spanish fishing fleet in exchange. Makes sense to me.

But there's one final thing that puzzles me. Why did they choose turbots over the Innu? Some back room politicking no doubt. Maybe the turbot have carried some influence in Ottawa. A fish lobby, perhaps? That's one school of thought. I've always figured there was something fishy happening in Ottawa.

Anything can happen there and usually does. I think somebody should check it out, you know, just for – dare I say it – the halibut.

Missionary Positions & Vegetarian Warriors

Recently a friend of mine, who works for a Native theatre company, was walking down a street to meet me for lunch. She was wearing the fur hat a family friend had given her. As she reached an intersection, a total stranger came up to her and snarled, "Do you realize you have a dead animal carcass on your head?" Surprised and a little frightened by this sudden and unwarranted antagonistic approach, my friend avoided a confrontation and went on her way. Later on during the meal, I suggested she should have responded with, "You have a dead animal carcass for a head."

The more I live in the city, the more I watch and read the media, the more I become amazingly aware of a disturbing fact of the dominating caucasian world. That is, very little in the philosophical practices of these people has changed over the centuries. The philosophies and goals have merely become different, become more 'politically correct,' but the method of achieving them still remains the same.

As the saying goes, "the more things change, the more they stay the same." I never really understood it – what it meant, the philosophical implications, the truth of it all. But as the years have gone by and I have observed more and more of the world around me, I have grown to understand the saying. At least a small part of it, anyways. And it scares me.

I refer to the dominant mentality that exists within western society. The overwhelming belief that what 'they' believe is correct, and what everybody else believes is wrong. I say "they" instead of "we" because in some ways I and my people are products of the implementation of these philosophies.

Most Canadians, hopefully, are aware of some of the tragic history of Native people. How we were forced to give up our land, forced into various Christian religions, forced into residential schools, forced onto reserves and forced by the government to give up children for adoption, and a hundred other 'forced to' all because the White race, in most cases (there are always exceptions I realize) has a firm belief that their way of doing things is the best and only way, and everybody should be forced to do or believe things that way, or they are not salvageable or welcome members of society. And in most cases, it is their duty to their 'cause,' be it political or religious or whatever, to enforce their beliefs, regardless of consequences on other people.

A big charge I know but easily proven: the Crusades, Spanish Inquisition, the conquest of the Americas, missionary work, Manifest Destiny, anti-semitism, White supremacists. Need I go on.

And as I stated, the beliefs that fuelled the passion exist today in many of the more socially-conscious causes.

Case in point: vegetarians. Now I have nothing against vegetarians, some of my best friends are vegetarians. I've been known to eat the odd vegetable myself, but some of these vegetarians have, I think, certain attitude problems. Some, when they see me eating a chicken leg or chomping on a roast beef sandwich, have this peculiar look that seems to be a combination of moral superiority and disgust. I know one person, who as a political protest to her meat-eating boyfriend, refuses to even walk down the meat aisle at the grocery store. But it goes way beyond that.

Several years ago I was working on a documentary series with a vegetarian producer. On our way back from a difficult day of shooting, the crew stopped off at a roadside diner for dinner late one night. Two of us sat at the counter with the producer. The crew member ordered fried chicken and no sooner had the words gotten out of her mouth when the producer proceeded, in graphic detail, to tell her about chicken farms.

I listened with a smile, having spent years being lectured to by well-meaning missionaries that came to our reserves with their own particular brand of truth.

As he finished, he caught me smiling and turned to me saying, "Not so fast. Now it's your turn." I got the 10-minute lecture on the evils of eating veal sandwiches. At least I learned one thing, never order veal in front of a vegetarian unless you want to piss him off. As I sat there, I was wondering if he actually thought he was making converts by doing this?

Regardless, it just made me relish the sandwich all the more, just out of spite. I hate it when people inform me that eating a simple sandwich is a political statement. If this keeps up, pretty soon I won't be allowed to have an English muffin until things change in Northern Ireland.

As a relatively well-read individual, I was already aware of what he was saying but I happened to have made the choice to eat meat, partly because I enjoy the taste, partly because it is part of my cultural heritage. But evidently a meat eater's choice isn't as well respected or logical as a vegetarian's choice. We are the enemy. How about those commercials done out west by k.d. lang urging people not to eat beef? A paid advertisement urging people to switch to their philosophy because theirs is better.

I know there are beef and pork commercials on T.V. too, but they are not suggesting vegetarians change their lifestyle to accommodate them. They are just urging, as is the way with advertising, meat eaters to try Ontario Beef or whatever. Two different standards because vegetarians think their lifestyle is morally and spiritually better.

A few months ago, my partner, a lapsed but struggling vegetarian, asked me to attend a lecture by a well-known vegetarian dietician and being open-minded, I went. Many of the things he had to say were accurate, healthy and made a lot of sense, but I still noticed a bit of mania in him. Something said to me, "This guy thinks he's right, and everybody is wrong."

"The human body isn't made to eat meat. It destroys the body rather than builds it up. Nature has not made us carnivores." Tell that to all the Aboriginal tribes of North America, especially the northern nations whose diet consists mostly of meat. I'd like to see a vegetarian try and dig up a potato in three feet of snow. The Plains Indians survived almost totally on a diet of buffalo meat and they were amongst the strongest, healthiest people on the continent.

Another comment he made was about how the digestive tract has to draw calcium from bones in order to process the meat. He then goes on to say the "Eskimos" (which made me more suspicious of how accurate he was) have an incredibly high rate of osteoporosis. I know many people who have worked in the North, and Inuits themselves, and after asking some questions, nobody seems to know anything about this high rate of osteoporosis. I wonder why.

In fact, these people eat an amazing amount of animal flesh, some of it pure fat, yet for those that follow these traditional diets, they have a surprisingly low level of cholesterol and heart disease. Maybe nature did mean for them to eat meat. Could it possibly be that this particular vegetarian was wrong?

And often times these same people belong to the animal rights organizations. A worthwhile organization within its own right, yes. Nobody wants to see animals suffer, but not when the organization sets out to destroy the ways of a people who have lived peacefully with and harvested the bounty of the land longer than the immigrant culture has been on this continent. I think not.

Just recently I saw a character on *Saturday Night Live* throw a bucket of paint on an image of someone wearing a fur coat, actively promoting his belief that fur is wrong. Throwing paint on someone you disagree with?! Now there's a sophisticated political doctrine I'd like to follow. Surely evidence of a superior civilization. No doubt members of the Church of the

Divine Spray Can.

Several years ago, when the boycott against seal fur came into effect, it wasn't just coats from Newfoundland seal pups that were affected. But all seal products from all over the Arctic. People that had nothing to do with that whole mess suffered as a result. But certain people were convinced that if one branch of the tree is bad, you should cut the whole tree down. As a result, Inuit communities in the north were devastated. It was no longer economically viable to hunt seals, even for food. The bullets and the gas for their outboard motors to hunt seal cost too much to make the hunt worth it.

Instead, many communities experienced a horrendous increase in criticism about the Aboriginal way of life. Another example of non-Native people making sure everybody follows their rules.

Another example of moral superiority is certain aspects of the philosophy behind Feminism. When I started seeing my partner Marie, who describes herself as a 'woman who advocates feminism' she was asked by her friend, someone she describes as a 'radical feminist,' if I was 'conscious.' By whose standards? Hers? Evidently this is a term used to characterize someone who believes their particular socio-political agenda.

As someone who was raised by a hard-working, single mother, and brought up in a culture that has a traditional respect and reverence for women, I find that term 'conscious' a little presumptuous. And from what I understand, this radical feminist looked a little disappointed when Marie, answering her question, told her no, not in the western sense. I refuse to be a card-carrying anything. But when her friend found out I was Native, she sighed a breath of relief, uttering, "At least you're both oppressed." Marie happens to be Filipino. I am to assume the only saving grace she could find in me was the fact I was 'oppressed?' Nothing else about me mattered, only that?

If I understand all this correctly, only certain people, an

incredibly small fraction of the world's population who believe in western feminism, can be classified as 'conscious,' What are the rest of us who don't follow to the letter these beliefs for the most part created and followed by middle-class White women of privilege? Are the rest of us perhaps unconscious, or subconscious maybe?

Somebody once asked me if I, because I was dating Marie, was going to become a Feminist? I said sure, when Marie becomes a Native person. We respect each other's beliefs and convictions – Marie is now quite well-known in Native artistic circles and I have often accompanied her to and supported many of her feminist causes.

And does the term 'consciousness' only refer to feminism? If so, that's awfully bold of them to appropriate that word. I'm tempted to go up to these people and ask "Are you conscious? Do you know about Native beliefs or Native issues?" Is that allowed?

But to me, the most obvious example of "my way of life is better than your way of life" is Sunday morning television. There you see wall-to-wall television evangelism. People screaming at you to believe only in their way of worshipping God, and nobody else's. To me this exemplifies this whole attitude.

These people have made a career out of telling others to follow their way of doing things, or risk going to hell. Their creed, their dogma is the better way. Sound familiar?

You never see Native people on television preaching about the benefits of their religion. As you're eating your scrambled eggs on Sunday morning, you don't see an Ojibway Elder shouting out to pray to the Four Directions, and to send in $50 for some traditional sweetgrass so you too can have your own cleansing ceremony. When's the last time you saw a Native person going door to door trying to convince you to come to a sweat lodge?

It's not our way. The Native way, the Native belief is to basically say, "you're more than welcome to join us in what we do, but you don't have to if you don't want to. You have your way, we have ours." I don't see that a lot outside of Native circles. Take the abortion issue for example – both sides screaming at each other, actually coming to physical blows because each thinks they are morally right, and the other side is morally wrong. Again, sound familiar?

Now this is not to say people are not entitled to their opinions. Everybody has them, and everybody should. But I, as an individual and a Native person, don't appreciate having other people 1) tell me my lifestyle or beliefs are wrong, or 2) they have a better way for me to live or that their opinions are better than mine.

And I am well aware that not every single person in today's society may have this driven state of mind, but enough do to make life for the rest of us difficult.

I myself, like everyone else, have my own political and philosophical agenda I live by, but who the hell am I to say my viewpoint, my lifestyle choices are better than anybody else's? That would be very arrogant to me. So, please, feel free to ignore everything I've just said. Heaven forbid, I wouldn't want to possibly influence anybody.

THE FIRST NAIL IN DIAND'S COFFIN

Ding dong, the department's dead. Which old department? The mean old department.

Well, maybe it's not dead yet, merely ill, on it's last legs, about to kick the proverbial bureaucratic can, suffering from chronic archaism and terminal outdatedness. I am, of course referring to the soon-to-be-late Department of Indian Affairs. I would say "let us observe a moment of silence," but I hear people out on the reserves cheering much too loudly. No more forms to fill out or offices to visit, or people to tell you what you can and can't do, or who is a Native and who isn't. In my mind's eye I can see river upon river clogged with discarded Indian Status cards.

Just a few weeks ago, strangely enough on the anniversary of Pearl Harbour, Federal Indian Affairs Minister Ron Irwin set in motion the machinery that will see to the department's own obsolescence. By signing an agreement with Manitoba Grand Chief Phil Fontaine that will allow individual Native communities more autonomy, the DIA has effectively put the first nail in its coffin.

Native people looking after Native people. What a concept. Talk about the ultimate in political correctness. Just a few years ago, the term 'Indian' was deemed inaccurate and offensive and the expression was soon put out to pasture. Now, the whole Department of Indian Affairs as well as the Indian Act are as passe as their names, and are about to be taken out to a government field somewhere and a bullet put through their jurisdictional heads.

I don't mean to sound bitter, but you can't grow up Native

in this country without feeling a certain animosity towards this big overwhelming and faceless government organization that was set up specifically to run your life. And I have always marvelled at what a misnomer the name Department of Indian Affairs was itself.

As a child I always had visions of people in turbans from India running around having affairs with each other. You can imagine my disappointment when I managed to get a job there eons ago and discovered the boring reality of working in a DIA office. Talk about a let-down.

And did you know, the Indian Act is one of the few pieces of government legislation in the world that actually and precisely defines what a specific race of people is and how they fit into the scheme of society? Scary, huh?

Oh well, the end of those days is within sight. Oh sure, there will be some birthing pains, there always are with things like this. But look at South Africa. Canadian reserves and the DIA eerily mirrored the now abolished apartheid system. While Phil Fontaine isn't exactly my idea of Nelson Mandela – Mandela dresses better – it's got to start somewhere.

RAMA-LAMA DING DONG

There is a certain irony afoot in the playing fields of Central Ontario. One mired in historical significance.

On July 31, 1996, a new god had arrived near the town of Orillia, ready to take its place amongst the heavens of the Ojibway dogma. A god, strangely enough, borrowed from the pantheon of Hindu deties. The irony is that the Hindu religion got its beginnings in India, where as history would teach us, Columbus thought he landed when he hit the Caribbean. So, the Indians have a new god from India. God does have a sense of humour.

I am of course talking about the Rama Reserve, and its brand spanking new gambling casino. In Eastern teachings, the name Rama is a manifestation of the Hindu God Vishnu the Creator, and I'm sure the people who are running the casino at Rama are hoping this new enterprise will "create" lots of money, jobs and various other forms of prosperity for the community. Evidently there are already Gambling Anonymous chapters being set up to assist some of the shall we say, more enthusiastic followers of this new religion.

To echo the name Vishnu the Creator, I think we should call this place Rama the Casino, because it has everything a new faith requires to be considered legitimate. For example, an estimated 14,000 new converts are expected everyday to pass through the halls of worship. Some religions require people to donate a percentage of their income to the church as a sign of devotion. No problem with that in Rama. In fact, that's why most of the disciples are there in the first place.

Many local artists have adorned the walls of the holy

Casino with Native art depicting various preceptions of Aboriginal spirituality, the equivalent of stained glass windows. No doubt something to gaze at while throwing the spiritual dice. And as the devoted are no doubt aware, the circle in Native mythology has a certain amount of reverence, as in the circle of life. Another staple of the Aboriginal cannon is the number four, as in the four directions and the four seasons.

Rama the Casino abounds in both types of reverence. Witness the round roulette wheel and ball, the circular chips used to play with, the four edged playing cards, the four sides of the dice table, even the building has four sides. It must be devinely inspired. But I, myself, am dubious about this new faith. It seems to be the latest in a long line of new religions embraced by Naitve people. Like most religions, it could be good, it might not be. Gambling, like life, is a crap shot. But perhaps this situation requires a little more research. The bus for the holy halls of Rama the Casino leaves at three. I'll let you know.

2
Mirror, Mirror on the Wall

AN ABORIGINAL NAME CLAIM

Recently I was innocently and harmlessly strolling through the newly reopened Art Gallery of Ontario when I looked up. Looked waaaayyy up. There, towering at least twenty-five feet or so above me, was a huge word carved into immutable stone. The word, Ojibway, is the Aboriginal nation I'm just lucky enough to be a member of. And around that incredible noble tribe inscribed forever upon that wall, were a half dozen other words, naming various Native tribes from throughout Ontario. So I thought to myself on that unusual day, "Now this is something you don't see everyday."

By unusual I mean you don't see the name Ojibway printed in public that noticeably unless it's on the front page of a newspaper with the phrases like 'land claim' or 'mass suicide' attached somewhere. Growing up, I used to think phrases like that were all one word. For instance, 'Ojibway Land Claim.' That's usually the only time you would see that word unless you were an anthropologist, archeologist, government official, or lacrosse player.

So we kids would run around the reserve yelling out to our friends "Hey, how's your Ojibway Land Claim?" "I hear Running Arrow (his real name was Bill) has got a new Ojibway Land Claim. Cool!" "I bet my Ojibway Land Claim is bigger than yours!" Ah, the wonders of youth.

So there I stood, in the Art Gallery of Ontario, looking up at that majestic looking word hovering high above me, thinking "Sure is nice. Clean looking too. Even spelled it right. Pity the word's wrong." Perhaps the word 'wrong' is a little too harsh, because I know that is the term that most Canadians are familiar with. Let's just say it's become...antiquated. With Native culture flourishing in its renaissance, more Native words are actually being used to describe Native things. What an interesting concept.

This is a fascinating reversal of history since for the longest time, Native names were used to describe things that weren't very Native. 'Canada' for instance, or the word 'Toronto.' How many 'Canadians' think of Native people when they hear the word 'Toronto?' Probably about as many people as think of our Wisconsin Native brothers when they hear the word 'Winnebago.'

And Frobisher Bay is now called Iqaluit and so on. Now a days, no self-respecting Ojibway-type supporter of the Cultural Rebirth would use that term. Most Ojibways prefer to be known as the Anishnawbe. Say it with me – the Anishnawbe.

This is because Ojibway is not really what we call ourselves. This is a name that has been foisted upon us poor unsuspecting Anishnawbe. The origins of that questionable word are kind of hazy but there are several schools of thoughts on that word and how we came to be called that.

According to the all-knowing and all-curious anthropologists who are so fascinated with us, the word Ojibway translates into something to do with the term 'puckered.' Now, while the majority of Ojibways are fantastic kissers (and I can attest to that), I mean puckered in a different context. The first theory has to do with moccasins. Now supposedly the Anishnawbe had a very distinctive way of sewing the seams on their moccasins that give it a certain 'puckered' appearance. If this is true, the entire contemporary Anishnawbe Nation may have to change its name to the noble Reebox First Nation.

The other, somewhat more grisly explanation, has to do with the way human skin puckers up when it's being burned alive. Now, scholars who claim this don't seem to be sure if we were the burners or the burnees, and frankly, I'm not sure which is worse. But that would explain my mother's fondness for bar-b-ques. So there you go. Scientists believe we were named after shoes or burning human skin. There's a proud choice.

Obviously, certain Native academics disagree with this interpretation of history (now there's a surprise). According to 'Ojibway' writer and cultural historian Basil Johnston, the word 'Ojibway' is actually a bastardization of a Cree word describing the Anishnawbe people as 'those who stutter.' It seems, evidently, the Cree are a very proud nation who consider themselves to be elegant speakers of the language and enunciate their words perfectly. But, in their opinion, the Anishnawbe mangle the language and mumble their words. Thus we were labeled 'those who stutter.' Thanks a lot, guys.

The Iroquois, on the other hand deemed it necessary to refer to us as the 'Adirondacks,' or so I've been told. Not because we were big and strong like the same-named mountain range, but because, as the name translates, we were bark eaters. Historically the Anishnawbe used to peel certain types of bark and stuff it into rabbits and ducks as they cooked. This bark was loaded with Vitamin C and helped prevent scurvy. Or in times of winter hardship, all that would be available to eat would be mosses and bark brewed into teas.

None of these names by other nations are exactly flattering. That's why I prefer the name we call ourselves. Anishnawbe means 'the good beings' or 'the people.' And not burning ones either. Just regular pass-the-tea-what's-for-dinner-who-are-the-Leafs-playing-tonight type people.

And to tell you the truth, that works out just wonderfully for me. I'd rather be known as a good being than a bark-eating-mumbling-human-burning-puckered shoe any day. Unless the shoe is a Bata. Then we're talking serious money.

An Indian by any other Name

Last week I, a reasonably well educated man of the ever more complex 90's, made a tremendous political and social faux pas. I made the terrible mistake of referring to myself, and other people of my ethnic background as 'Indians.' Oh the shame of it all. You could hear the gasp echo across the room. It was done, I assure you, in the most innocent of intention, but nevertheless, I was soon castigated by both my brethren and, in my humble opinion, the overly politically sensitive members of other Native groups. And the White people! Needless to say, in these politically correct times, I was soon inundated by these same people with criticisms about my use of such an outdated term. "We're/You're no longer called Indians!" I was told over and over again.

Evidently I am in severe error for responding to that term for the last 31 years. No doubt an oversight on my part, and my entire family, and my reserve, not to mention the vast majority of the country. Growing up in school, all us were proud to be 'Indians.' It had a certain power to it that set us aside from all the White kids (or should I say Children of Occidental Decent). Somehow the cry of 'Proud to be Indigenous Population' just doesn't have the same ring. Or picture this, you arrive thirsty in some new town, and you ask the first skin you see, "Yo, neechee, where's the nearest First Nations Bar?" Sorry, just doesn't work for me.

I guess I'm out of date? Oh I understand the reasoning behind all the hubbub. Columbus, a member of the European/Caucasian Nation, thought he had found India and all that. That's cool, but there's also another school of thought that says that Columbus was so impressed by the generosity and gentleness of the Native population of the Caribbean, he wrote back to Spain that they were "of the body of God" or in Spanish, 'corpus in dea.' In deo – Indian. A pretty thin link, but who knows? I knew some Indians with God-given bodies.

But a person in my position doesn't have to defend himself with theoretical history. I was too busy handling the deluge. By deluge I mean the flood of politically correct terms I was permitted and urged to use following my faux pas.

It must be obvious to most people that in the last couple of years Native people in Canada have gone through an enormous political metamorphosis, similar to what people of African decent did in the United States. Years ago they used to be called Niggers, then Negro, then Coloured, then Black and finally today, I believe the correct term is African-American or African-Canadian.

That's nothing compared to the choice selection of current names and categories available to the original inhabitants of this country. And these names or classifications have nothing to do with any tribal affiliations either. These are just generic terms used to describe us 'Indians.' Grab some aspirin and let me give you some examples.

First of all, let's start with the basics. Status, non-Status, Metis. So far painless. I guess next would come the already mentioned Indian, followed by Native, Aboriginal, Amerindian, Indigenous and First Nations. Pay attention, there's going to be an exam later. From there we can go to on-Reserve, off-Reserve, urban, treaty. Got a headache yet? How about the enfranchised Indians, the Bill C-31 or reinstated people, the traditional Indians, the assimilated Indian? I'm not finished yet. There are the wannabe's (the White variety), and of course the ever popular full bloods. My personal favourites are what I call the Descartes Indians, "I think Indian, therefore I am Indian."

Get the picture? Right there are two dozen separate names for our people. Where does it all stop? I wanna know who keeps changing all the rules? Even I get confused sometimes.

That's why I usually use the term 'Indian.' I'm just too busy or too lazy to find out which way the political wind is blowing or to delve deeply into the cultural/governmental background of who I'm talking to or writing about. By the time I go through all the above mentioned categories, I've missed my deadline. Then I become an unemployed Indian.

But I know what your thinking. Why should I listen to this guy? What the hell does he know? He's just probably some Status, off-reserve, urban, Native, Aboriginal, treaty, half-breed Indian. This week anyway.

What Colour is a Rose?

As a Native writer there are always three questions I get asked, ad nauseam, when ever I do a lecture or a reading for a non-Native audience. Question one: "What do you feel about cultural appropriation?" My answer: "About the same as I feel about land appropriation." Question two: "When you write your plays or stories, do you write for a specifically Native audience or a White audience?" My answer: "I'm usually alone in my room when I write, except for my dying cactus. So I guess that means I write for my dying cactus." The final and in my opinion, most annoying question I often get asked is "Are you a writer that happens to be Native, or a Native that happens to be a writer?"

I was not aware there had to be a difference. I was always under the impression that the two could and often were synonymous. But evidently I am in error. Over the past few years working as a professional writer, I have slowly began to understand the rules of participation in the television and prose industry in terms of this difference. It seems there is a double standard. Surprise, surprise.

It is not uncommon, though deemed politically incorrect, for White writers to write satires about Native people quite freely, particularly on television. Notice many of the 'people of pallor' script credits on such shows such as *North of Sixty* (which, granted, does have one talented Native writer), *Northern Exposure* (I guess I'll have to move north since it seems that's where all the Native people live), movies like *Where the Spirit Lives* or the upcoming *Dance Me Outside*. All these shows have strong identifiable Native characters created by non-Natives.

However, should a Native writer want to explore the untroddened world outside the Aboriginal literary ghetto, immediately the fences appear, and opportunities dry up. Evidently, the powers that be out there in the big cruel world have very specific ideas of what a Native writer can and can't do. Only recently a friend of mine submitted a story to a new CBC anthology series in development, about Native people, called *The Four Directions*.

His story outline was soon returned with an explanation that the producers thought the story wasn't "Native enough" for their purposes. I myself submitted a story to the producers and during our first story meeting, I received a stirring and heartfelt lecture about how they, the producers, were determined to present the Native voice as authentically and accurately as possible, and how committed they were to allowing us Native-types the chance to tell our stories our way. Then asked if I could cut the first eight pages of my 27 page script. Oddly enough, they seemed puzzled by my sudden burst of laughter.

I once wrote an episode of *Street Legal* and I accidently caught a glimpse of a memo from the producer to a story editor asking him to rewrite the dialogue of my Native Elder to "make him more Indian." I guess as a Native person, I don't know how real 'Indians' talk. Bummer. These are just a few examples of the battle Native writers often face.

I hereby put the question to these people who judge our stories. I personally would like to know by what set of qualifications these people examine Native stories. Is there an Aboriginal suitability quotient posted somewhere? If there is, I would love the opportunity to learn more about how I should write as a Native person.

For a story to be "Native enough" must there be a birch bark or buckskin quota? Perhaps there is supposed to be vast roaming herds of moose flowing past the screen. Oh geez, I guess I'm not Native enough. I momentarily forgot, moose don't herd, they just hang out with flying squirrels that have their own cartoon show.

Or maybe I's got be good writer like dem Indians whats W.P. Kinsella writes about. It no sound like any Indian I ever hears but what the hell, I maybe win bunch of awards. On second thought, you never mind. I get headache trying write like this.

So what's a writer to do? Damned if he does, damned if he doesn't. And what if I want to write stories about non-Native people? It's possible, but will I be given a chance? I'm sure I could do it. I've learned enough about how White people really live from watching all those episodes of *Married With Children* and *Baywatch*.

This all brings us back to my original question. Am I a writer who happens to be Native or a Native that happens to be a writer? Do I have a choice? I think that the next time I get asked that question, I'll ask the equally deep and important question – "Is a zebra black with White stripes, or White with black stripes?"

Just watch. They'll make that into a racial question.

CALL OF THE WEIRD

When I first read the job description for the position of Artistic Director of Native Earth Performing Arts, Toronto's only professional Native theatre company, I don't remember coming across any paragraph or subsection anywhere on the page requiring me to become the "oracle of the Aboriginal trivia."

On any given day, questions of unusual and frequently surreal nature are posed to me and the other intelligent, though often puzzled, members of the office. The number of times I've seen heads, with telephones attached, shaking in amazement, makes me wonder about the logical processes of people's minds.

We are a theatre company. That is what we do. We produce plays by and about Native people. Check it out, it's in our mandate. We'll fax it to you if you don't believe us. The majority of questions that Bell Canada sends our way are not within our realm of expertise. While one of our functions as a theatre company is to educate the public, that does not mean one at a time, about obscure issues, while our other work waits. We have lives too, you know.

Our beleaguered office staff has put together a collection of some of the more...interesting...inquires to come through our office in recent months.

I'm trying to find Sam Ke-something or other. I really don't know how to pronounce his last name. Do you know where I can find him? Or, I'm trying to locate a Bob Whitecloud of the Sioux Tribe in the States. I heard he might be in Canada. Can you tell me how to get in touch with him?

It's a little known fact that Native Earth Performing Arts

is the focal point for all Native people in North America. The one million or so people claiming some sort of Aboriginal ancestry all pass through our doors at one point or another. That's why we have to replace our carpets at least four times a year.

Do all the seats face the stage?

I guess you can call us slaves to conformity. We did try having the seats face the back of the theatre but audience reaction, shall we say, was not that favourable.

Hi, I'm wondering if you can help me. I'm to locate an Apache wedding prayer.

I checked. Sorry, no Apaches in our office, married or not. I did however manage to find a Mohawk secret handshake.

I'm with a casting company for a movie. I'm looking for a Native man, tall and lean with long dark hair and presence. Preferably he should be in his early 30's. And yes, he has to look very striking.

Yeah, most of the women in my office are looking for him too. What do you want me to do about it? The line starts behind them.

I'm phoning from Edinburgh, Scotland. I'm doing research on Native people in the 1930's. Can you send me information?

There were none. I have it on good authority all Native people were killed off in the late 1800's. But in the latter part of this century, due to an over abundance of bureaucrats in Ottawa, the Federal government decided to create a new department to employ these people. So the Department of Indian Affairs was created with no Indians. Through secret DNA experiments, a new race of Native people was created at a clandestine location known as...Algonquin Park.

I'm Herman ---------- from Germany. I'm looking for people of the Bear clan. My last name means bear in German. Do you know any or can you help me find the Bear clan?

Sorry, we have yet to update our data base and cross reference our membership, actors, directors, stage managers and others by clan affiliation. We're awaiting for the software to come out for Windows.

We're an organization of men against men who commit violence against women. We want to know if you guys could provide any ceremonies or spiritual things of that nature that would help us with healing and matters like that.

While that is a noble cause, we are not 'Ceremonies 'R' Us,' or 'have medicine pouch, will travel.'

Do you know where I can get my hands on some Inuit throat singers?

As a Native organization, we do not condone violence against the Inuit.

In all fairness and honesty, we do try to be as polite and helpful as possible, and pass callers on to the appropriate organizations. But we are in the business of making art, not making a Native trivial pursuit game. But it makes me wonder if the Mirvishes ever get calls asking, "there's this Jewish song I keep hearing. Hava-something. You wouldn't happen to know the full title and who sang it would you?"

Coloured Movies: Aboriginals on Parade

The latest in the "I'm so fascinated by Indians I just have to make a film about them" movie opens on March 10. *Dance Me Outside*, directed by Bruce Macdonald, pieces together several W.P. Kinsella short stories (how Altmanesque) into quite a wonderfully shot and acted film detailing the life of a couple of down-home Rez boys and girls. Politics and accuracy aside, the film hits on many levels.

But more than anything, it's another example of Hollywood and its' Canadian equivalent increasing preoccupation with Natives and their ways of life. Even Disney is coming out with an elaborate cartoon version of *Pocahontas*. I hear her guardian spirit will be a large mouse.

Andy Warhol used to say everybody will be famous for 15 minutes. If you're Indian, you can count on a call from the coast, babe, and bring your shades. You're not signing the contract until you get at least a good 90 minutes, with an option for a sequel. "Have your Indian agent call me."

And when they say they want their own Winnebago, they're talking about the tribe in Wisconsin.

With so many films about Native people having come out in the last few years, it's hard to keep track of which ones are good, and which ones should be shot with a burning arrow and left to die on an ant hill.

I, however, have some suggestions:

Dances With Wolves – The granddaddy of them all. Kevin Costner's epic homage to the romantic Indian. A beautifully shot and conceived film but I have to admit, I kept looking for someone in the film to say, "I never met an Indian I didn't like." Since its premiere many winters ago, the film has taken on a sort of mythic quality, the way *Star Wars* did for sci-fi films. If that's true, I'm waiting for all the little Lt. John Dunbar and Wind In His Hair action figures.

Pow Wow Highway – An absolutely marvellous little film starring A. Martinez and Gary Farmer, with executive producer ex-Beatle George Harrison. An old fashioned road movie, sort of a healthily tanned comedic version of *Of Mice and Men*. Simply put, a story of redemption and pride, of Gary Farmer in a bad wig, and A. Martinez scowling better than anybody I know. Once you see this film, you'll have a whole new respect for your car.

Black Robe – Never saw it. Didn't want to see it. Read the book. That was the reason why I didn't want to see it. But thanks to this movie, our biggest secret is now out. Yes, it's true. Indians do have sex. And the fact it was with religious missionaries was oddly prophetic of future events, like residential schools.

Clearcut – An awful movie starring the amazing Graham Greene. I remember being asked to read the script for a funding agency and thinking to myself as I read it, "you've got to be kidding?" Graham Greene kidnaps a White journalist and industrialist and proceeds to torture and do all sorts of despicable things that only a Native person can do. And there's also the implication he might be a spirit. The Native community is full of spirits. You can't swing a dead beaver without hitting a spirit.

Last of the Mohicans – The great looking story of great looking White people and great looking Indians in a great looking forest. Directed by Michael Mann, the guy who gave us *Miami Vice*. It's a great looking movie. I don't remember my history teacher telling me the French-Indian wars were this great looking.

Thunderheart – It has everything a good Hollywood story should have: drama, a love story, a car chase, a mysterious murder, intrigue, and Graham Green. Val Kilmer and his faithful Indian companion (boy, that sounds familiar) search for murderers in 'the fourth world,' a Sioux Reservation. Loosely based on real incidents surrounding Leonard Peltier and events at the Pine Ridge Reservation, this film however, has a fairly happy ending. If only art did imitate life.

Shadow of the Wolf – The resident Hollywood Indian, Lou Diamond Phillips makes a stab at being Inuit this time, with his Inuit wife, Jennifer Tilly and Inuit father, Toshiro Mifune(!?). One of the most expensive Canadian films made, it disappeared like the Arctic sun in wintertime. While made as a serious drama, a friend of mine who lived in the Arctic for two years actually found it to be a comedy.

On Deadly Ground – Steven Segal's attempt at directing and making a statement. The statement is this man should not direct. Seagal plays the stereotypical avenging White angel coming to save the poor Inuit people of Alaska from the evil oil men. I particularly loved the scene where he is having his 'vision' and he finds himself at a fork in a cave tunnel. One path leads to a beautiful, naked young lady undulating across a fur bed, the other path leads to an old, wise looking Elder who is staring at him. Being pure of spirit (having just killed a dozen people) he chooses the old woman. I guess he wasn't a missionary.

Geronimo – This film should be thrown from a plane without a parachute. A very dusty film that tries to boil down a dozen years into two hours and leaves you wondering, who cares? Made by the usually reliable Walter Hill, with a cast that boasts Wes Studi and Jason Patric as sympathetic adversaries in the deserts of the American Southwest. My favourite exchange – Wes Studi saying stoically, "I am Geronimo. Who are you?" Jason Patric as a cavalry lieutenant replying with a serious and intense whisper, "I'm a man. Just like you." Yep, that's what cavalry and Apaches used to say to each other all the time.

Maverick - While not exactly classified as a Native film, it does however feature the always-present Graham Greene, in standard Hollywood Aboriginal gear as a Native Mel Gibson, attitude-wise anyways. After seeing this film, I couldn't help wondering what this character was doing out in the bush dodging bullets when he could be a great stand-up comic. "Okay, a Cree, Sioux and Pawnee walked into a bar. The first one said..."

And by the way, did you know popcorn was invented by Native people? And the chocolate M&M's you eat and the Coke you drink are derived from the cocoa plant, another Native source. Going to the movies can be a positively Aboriginal experience.

Pocahontas: Beauty and the Belief

I must and will confess. I recently saw the Disney film *Pocahontas*. I was curious to see how the Land of Mickey would treat this all-American Native legend. Briefly, the music was naturally marketable, animation was, of course, fabulous, animals of the forest cute (though subconsciously you couldn't help thinking that Pocahontas's people made a regular habit of eating Bambi and Thumper), and it sort of confirmed the old adage, 'Never let facts get in the way of a good story'.

When John Smith first gets a good look at her, standing in the mist of a waterfall, her long black hair blowing and flowing sensuously in the wind (I wanna know what kind of hair conditioner she uses), her little off-the-shoulder buckskin dress hugging her body tightly (which is noticeably more cur- vaceous than Snow White, only goes to show you what a steady diet of Bambi and Thumper will do for you), you can't help but be a little uncomfortable knowing that the real Pocahontas wasn't much older than eleven or twelve years old when the whole thing came down with the Colonists.

Evidently, according to reports, she also 'amused' the Englishman by doing nude cartwheels through the colony. And from what I understand, there may even be some doubt as to whether John Smith and Pocahontas ever really met, let alone had any serious romantic relationship. But other than that, it was a good movie.

The whole Pocahontas legend can be looked at from sever- al different levels. First of all, it became the stuff great romances were made of. Check out any bookstore that has a sizable stock of historical romances. Count how many of them involve a forbidden romance between a Native person and a White person, and the fiery savage passions that smolders and threatens to break free beneath the taut leather. You get the picture.

When you look at the story objectively, it's about a romance between, at best, a 12-year-old Indian girl and a thirty-year-old sailor who was captured by Pocahontas' father. According to Smith, and only Smith's word, Pocahontas laid her head on his, openly defying her father, the Chief of the tribe, as Smith's head was about to be clubbed and crushed.

To quote the Native actress and playwright Monique Mojica's play, *Princess Pocahontas and the Blue Spots*, "where was this girl's mother?" To the best of my knowledge, this is not an activity most mother's would condone from a 12-year-old.

In the movie her mother is dead. But as we've already seen, this movie is not exactly big on historical accuracy.

If Pocahontas' mother had been around, no doubt she would have also warned her against falling for someone who says his name is John Smith. How many women have heard that before? And how many hotel rooms have this name scrawled on the register. Could it be this man is four hundred years old and still out there?

Both legend and Disney portray Smith to be a handsome, strapping blond-haired, blue-eyed man. This would explain why Pocahontas would fall for him, according to a theory of a Mohawk friend of mine. Over the years, he has come to believe that, for some reason, most Natives are attracted to shiny objects and like to collect them. This includes turquoise, silver, and blondes. That's something for a sociologist or anthropologist to ponder.

When all's said and done, Pocahontas (her real name, by the way, was actually Matoaka – Pocahontas was a nickname her father called her meaning "playful one") will make Disney a lot of wampum (which again in reality is not actually a form of Aboriginal currency), and this Christmas (its basically an accepted fact that Christ was not born on December 25), kids all over North America can expect a little American Indian princess doll (no doubt made somewhere in Asia). Sometime you just don't know what to believe.

Note: Pocahontas later converted to Christianity, married a colonist named John Rolfe, went to England, saw the original production of *The Tempest* just a few weeks after the author died, and was consumed by small pox at the age of 22.

WAITING FOR KINSELLA

It was the showdown that never happened. The case of the missing confrontation. Though it seemed, at least to me, like the media built it up to be something potentially and politically volatile, I must confess that it died with a whimper, not a bang. I am, of course, talking about my appearance at Toronto's International Festival of Authors, with the most notable of alleged Aboriginal cultural appropriators, W.P. Kinsella.

Speaking as an Ojibway playwright and Artistic Director of Native Earth Performing Arts, Toronto's only professional Native theatre company, it seemed it was expected of me to face the man from the west, armed with only baseball bats (his advantage) or lacrosse sticks (my advantage). But showdown at the W.P. Corral it wasn't.

The day I saw my name on the brochure of invited writers, a dozen or so authors after Kinsella, I knew this festival wasn't going to be as much fun as I had anticipated. I felt the potential cultural storm beginning to blow in. Already, many of my Native friends were attempting to generate within me a murderous literary froth; an Indigenous intellectual rage; urging an Aboriginal jihad for lack of a better term. I was getting the impression this festival wasn't big enough for the two of us.

The media were no help. I did three interviews concerning the festival. First question. "So Drew, excited about the festival?" Second question. "Tell me about Native theatre/literature in Canada." Third question. "Cultural appropriation. Kinsella's gonna be there. Comments?"

When asked a question, I always try to be polite and

answer it. Yes, I do have opinions on the whole Kinsella thing. Yes, I have read his stories and while I consider him a gifted storyteller, he obviously doesn't write his Native stories with the same kind of love he puts into his baseball tales. Anybody who's read both and compared them can tell. And if there's no love involved in the stories you tell, why tell them? But I repeat, I am NOT gunning for Kinsella.

So there I am, being polite and answering these searing journalistic questions (must have been a slow day at the O.J. trial), and this stuff starts popping up in print, on radio and television. MuchMusic even did some sort of head to head debate between me and Kinsella by interviewing us at differ-ent times, asking us the same questions, and intercutting between the two of us. I haven't seen it but I'm told it looked like an interesting debate.

It all came to a not-spectacular head one night at one of the social functions for the festival. I arrived somewhat late for the festivities. I had no sooner walked in the door when two publicists, within a dozen seconds of each other, came rac-ing over to me and quickly but quietly whispered in my ear, "Kinsella's here!" My first reaction was "So what?"

I looked across the crowded room at where they were pointing and saw him – a tall, thin chap with long blondish hair, mustache and beard, a cowboy hat, and a striped shirt with a western bolo tie. He looked vaguely familiar. I could-n't place the memory but something about it seemed tinged with irony.

If by some chance we were placed in a conversational posi-tion, I had no idea what I would say to him. One Native writer friend suggested that I tell him he can't write. Not only would that have been rude, but in my opinion, inaccurate. The man can write, but it's his choice and treatment of subject matter that I would question. Another person, urging I remain neutral and nonconfrontational, suggested I talk to him about baseball.

However, there is no baseball to talk about and the game

is about as important to me as Native self-government probably is to him. But these are now moot points.

To this day, even with all the press, I have absolutely no
idea if he knows who I am. But during the entire festival (and
I'm sure it was completely by accident), we never ended up sitting at the same table for dinner, or perchance talking together. My entire contact with him consisted of squeezing by him
in a crowded room on my way to the bathroom. Our conversation involved a grand total of two scintillating words
"Excuse me."

Instead, the week passed and the man has long since left.
I'm sure he's a nice man. And I'm sure he's as sick and tired
of this whole damn thing as I am. So contrary to rumours you
may have heard, I have not put a contract out on him or
placed an ancient Ojibway curse on him. I figure anybody who
looks and dresses like George Armstrong Custer (I remembered) is a marked man anyways.

WHATEVER HAPPENED TO BILLY JACK?

I don't know about all people but to me, political revelation is often inspired by the strangest places. As usual, it was another lonely Friday night, the kind I've been seeing much too regularly. And in those wee morning hours I sat on my couch in front of the television. I was munching on a bowl of popcorn lightly seasoned with low fat margarine, when an image I remembered from my childhood flashed across the screen. There, sandwiched between phone sex commercials and offers for self-improvement videos and cassettes (interesting combination), stood Tom Laughlin, the famous Billy Jack to the common folk, the hero of my childhood.

You have to understand that in the early seventies there were precious few cinematic people for young impressionable Native kids to relate to. It was either him or Jesse Jim on the *Beachcombers*.

So there he was at the climax of the film, an Indian barricaded with his rifle, surrounded by multitudes of cops wanting to shoot him full of sizeable holes, yet managing to hold them off with superior skill and moral fibre. I understand they used to screen this movie every night at Oka.

His girlfriend enters the church and notices he's been shot. Stoic as all us Indians are in the movies, he ignores his bleeding side, saying quite melodramatically, "An Indian isn't afraid to die."

As I sat there munching on my popcorn, I thought "obviously we don't know the same Indians."

That's not of course to say that Native people are cowards or aren't willing to stand up for what they believe. As a Native person I know how quickly the Aboriginal people in this country are willing to take a stand no matter what the consequences. What I am referring to, instead, is the stereotypical impression characters like Billy Jack give to the world. Like we all appear mystically in the nick of time on our motorcycle/horse/jeep strutting around in our black T-shirts and black hats karate kicking White people in the side of head. Well...maybe a few, but generally you don't see too much of this on your average reserve.

As a Native person living in today's world, I am only too aware of false impressions a lot of people have of our Aboriginal society. I have yet to find one of these stereotypes that I fit into properly. I don't know, maybe my White blood throws the bell curve off or something. But I do know, dying isn't on my list of favourite things to do in the near future. Hopefully.

But in my experience, I've noticed four specific stereotypes that the majority of Native people are lumped into by the media. And because four is a special number in Native beliefs (i.e. the Four Directions) I like to call these the Four Sacred Stereotypes.

The first consists of the ever-popular sidekick syndrome. It seems it was impossible to get anything done without your trustworthy Indian companion like the Lone Ranger's Tonto, Nick's Jesse Jim, or Hawkeye's last two Mohicans. No wonder they were the last two Mohicans – they kept hanging around with a White guy instead of women.

The second is the fiery young Aboriginal radical, dedicated to saving his people whether they like it or not. Give him a soap box, a court room or a barricade and his spirit cries out against the injustices forced upon his people by the oppressive and dominant White society that for the centuries have been systematically draining the life blood out of... Well, you get the picture. Again Billy Jack kicks into action (literally).

The third is my personal favourite, the borderline psychotic, often drunk, out-of-control Indian who, given a chance, wouldn't hesitate to separate your spirit from reality quicker than you could dodge a bullet. Witness Arthur from *A Dream Like Mine*/*Clearcut*, 'Injun Joe from *Tom Sawyer* or the Indian from *Predator* or *48 Hours*. I like to call these people IWABA (Indians With A Bad Attitude).

Finally, we have the fourth stereotype, the mystical all-knowing Indian with one foot in the astral plane, the other in a canoe. You know the type, they melt in and out of the bush almost as effortlessly as they speak metaphorical wisdoms in poor English, about humanity and the world – without cracking a smile. You couldn't swing a dead cat without hitting that type of Indian on shows like *Little House on the Prairie*, *Grizzly Adams*, etc.

Or if the writer/director is feeling particularly adventurous, how about a psychotic, radical Elder sidekick?!

But like I said before, none of these descriptions really fit me. My best friend is Native so that sort of eliminates the sidekick syndrome. Perhaps we're two Indians in search of a White man? Now there's a scary thought.

I'm fairly certain I'm not the fiery radical type. While it is true being born Native in this country is a political act in itself, that's about the extent of it for me. I find radicals don't get paid nearly enough.

And as for the psychotic, angry drunk – being a writer is about as psychotic and angry as I can handle. As for me being out of control...talk to my mother.

Unfortunately I have some difficulty melting in and out of the bush magically. I've been told I have the unusual talent of being able to trip over footprints.

I sometimes wonder if there's a heaven for out-dated stereotypes, a place they all hang out when no longer in vogue. Somewhere out there is a card table with Tonto, Billy Jack, Uncle Remus, Shylock and the rest, playing cards to pass the time. I wonder if Billy's still wearing that black t-shirt and hat.

WHAT NATIVES WERE TALKING ABOUT IN 1993

As the world slowly creeps into the year 1994, it gives many of us the chance to reflect on the preceding year and its events. Upon examination, 1993 was an important year for the Aboriginal people of this country. There were many things to be proud of and pridefully show the world, but as seems to happen all too often in the Native world, many negative and tragic events seemed to dominate our community.

Add the fact it was also the International Year of Indigenous Peoples, a detail that was largely missed or ignored by the government and populace, and it all adds up to the conclusion that it was a very interesting year in more ways than one.

Alanis Obomsawin: Film maker Alanis Obomsawin's released her award winning documentary about Oka, Kanehsatake: 270 Years of Resistance. In the real world of cowboys and Indians, we salute Ms. Obomsawin for showing us who the bad guys actually were. I guess John Wayne is still dead.

Nunavut: It was announced that the Northwest Territories would be split into two separate political entities in 1999 – one for the Inuit and one for the non-Inuit. This occurred after the government just finished completing a brand new legislative assembly building in Yellowknife. Now they have to build another one in the Eastern Arctic. With self-government approaching, does that mean every reserve will get one?

Aboriginal Movies: In the entertainment world, Native people are still 'in.' Big Hollywood movies *Thunderheart* and *Geronimo* were released to lukewarm response. And a special mention should go out to the CBC for being economically minded by using practically the same Native casts for *North of Sixty, Medicine River*, and *Spirit Rider*. Who says Indians don't all look alike?

The Royal Commission on Aboriginal Peoples: Where is it? What's it done? Has it disappeared into the Ottawa Triangle with all the other commissions? Was Amelia Earhart the chairperson?

Political Biographies: The biographies of two Native politicians were released – Elijah Harper, who added a whole new dimension to Nancy Reagan's 'Just Say No' campaign and Ovide Mercredi, who did more for Indians in suits than when Graham Greene played a lawyer on *L.A. Law*. The two books contain just about everything you wanted to know about the men, the myths and the type of suits they wear. How far behind can the movie dramatization be? Elijah Harper, in his best Cree/Clint Eastwood accent asking "What part of 'no' don't you understand, punk?"

Suicide: The media covered the unfortunate cyclical rash of suicides and attempted suicides in communities like Davis Inlet. Some blame the suicides on the fact that they need a new community, preferably one that's livable (damn Indians, always wanting something!) Rumour has it that, for some strange reason, a healthy environment might actually cut down on the number of people wanting to kill themselves.

Smuggling: There was an explosion of interest in the underground economy of bootlegging. The flow of illegal cigarettes crossing the St. Lawrence at the Akwesasne Reserve caught the media's eye this year when the Cornwall mayor was allegedly shot at because of his request for a crackdown on the contraband trade. Well, they do say smoking is bad for you.

Religion: Manitoba Cree Stan McKay was named Moderator (head honcho) of the United Church of Canada for a two year term. Now there's something you don't often see – a Native person telling the church what to do.

Murder: The White supremist/RCMP informer who was convicted of shooting a Cree trapper as he left his store in downtown Prince Albert, Saskatchewan, was released after a little more than two years in jail. The murder resulted in a public inquiry that criticized the police and prosecutors for not recognizing the role racism may have played in the shooting. White supremist shoots Indian in back. Nope, no racism there. When all's said and done, Leo LaChance is still dead, and Carney Nerland has been given a new identity, a job, and probably a house in the RCMP's witness relocation program. Now what's wrong with this picture?

Thomas King: Native novelist Thomas King was nominated for the Governor General's Award for his wonderful, funny novel *Green Grass, Running Water.* It told the story of Indians, dams, legends, silliness, and general chaos. I guess White people would call it Parliament.

Jean Chretien: The federal election resulted in a new Prime Minister of Canada – Jean Chretien. In 1969, in his role as Indian Affairs Minister, Chretien orchestrated the infamous White Paper calling for the elimination of reserves and the end of all special status for Native people, which he said prevented them from becoming equal citizens of Canada. Supposedly he has since backtracked a bit on that stance but you know what they say about leopards and their spots. With a majority government, anything is possible. That's the thing about Canada, you never Know what can happen. If Leonard Cohen could win Best Male vocalist, don't be surprised if all us Indians are booted off the reserve and end up in your 'burbs looking for affordable split-level duplexes. Now there's a scary thought, for both sides.

NORTH OF SIXTY, SOUTH OF ACCURATE

I recently caught the season opener for *North of Sixty*, Canada's (via the CBC) view of Native people. And for a brief moment, I was surprised. There in front of me, for the grand total of about four, possibly five seconds, I thought I heard one of the characters utter a joke and then I actually saw somebody smile. I was amazed. What has always been one of the more somber shows on television, for a brief moment let us see some genuine Native soul.

When the show first went into production several years ago, there was great excitement in the Native community. There had been a few attempts by the television industry to capture the essence of Aboriginal life, some successful, some not. The *Beachcombers* had several permanent cast members of Native descent, but seldom did the stories deal with their issues. In the mid-eighties there was a family show called *Spirit Bay* that dealt with Native kids growing up on a reserve. All in all, this show was enjoyable, though kind of light. But all journeys begin with the first step.

Then, after a long drought came *North of Sixty*, a show taking place in an actual Aboriginal community (albeit reconstructed), with the majority of characters being Native, except for that pesky White central character that all shows about Native people seem to need (the concept being audience identification). Even then, it quickly became apparent to the story editors that the story possibilities for this one character had became exhausted by the seventh or eighth episode, and gradually the focus of the show began to shift to the more interesting Native characters in the community.

With four years under its belt, the show has had some

interesting hits and some conspicuous misses. It has provided a solid vehicle for introducing the amazing talents of Tina
Keeper, Tom Jackson, Tina Louise Bomberry, Gordon
Tootoosis and the rest of the fictional Lynx River to the
Canadian public. Practically every working Native actor in
Canada and parts of the U.S. have found themselves in some
sort of pickle in the Northwest Territories. The show also has
a fine reputation for training Native people in story editing
and other television jobs.

For the most part, it has acquainted the television audience with the multi-faceted lives of Aboriginal people of
Canada. Issues that were only statistics now have faces, voices, and reasons. Perhaps this is also the show's biggest weak-
ness – it's preoccupation with and dedication to showing the
negative aspects of Aboriginal life. When the first show aired,
I became a faithful viewer, tuning in to see how long the
Mountie would survive in this community. I related to Teevee,
having had the same fixation with television, pop culture, and
the world outside at his age.

Each episode became a tour-de-force for dysfunctionalism.
In an average season topics such as alcoholism, infidelity, residential school abuse, and teenage pregnancy were endured by
this little Dene community in the North. What at first was
hailed as a breakthrough, now concerns a lot of Native people. Canadian viewers were seeing Lynx River as the most
dysfunctional community (outside of soap operas) on Canadian
television. There was a growing concern that the show
endorsed the perpetuation of Natives as victims.

The more I watched the show, especially Teevee's efforts
to leave the community, and all the horrible things that
were happening around him, I was tempted to take up a collection to buy the poor kid a plane ticket to get him the hell
out of there. No wonder he is such a pain. I would be too if
I lived under the same circumstances.

Admittedly, it's easy to be critical but I don't stand alone.
I did an informal poll on my reserve. Alice Williams, born in

Northern Ontario, now living in Curve Lake First Nations, shares a similar opinion. She feels the show "confirms, affirms and promotes dominant culture ideology about the Anishnawbe (Native people)." A health worker in the community agrees, saying "it's all doom and gloom, too depressing for me."

One Native academic I met in Sudbury pointed out an interesting tendency in the show. Though it is essentially a show about Native people, the central character is the White Mountie, and the other White people seem to be in all the important positions of power in the community. One is the Band Manager who handles all the money, the other runs the only store and motel in the village. And then there was the nurse, until she went nuts. They all seem to be 'looking after' the local Native people.

The White nurse also inspired an interesting theory from my academic friend. He says Gordon Tootoosis, the village's bootlegger, became chief of the community twice – once when he was elected chief, and again when he started a relationship with the beautiful blonde nurse (an icon of White civilization). And she wasn't even a good icon. She had a nervous break-down, indicating that Tootoosis' character was only good enough to get a defective icon.

Rodney Bobiwash, director and agent provocateur of the First Nations House at the University of Toronto, often cites *North of Sixty* in his lectures. As an anti-racism consultant for the Native Canadian Centre of Toronto, Bobiwash is a frequent speaker on the lecture circuit. He says the show is "shucking and jiving to the Native beat. I don't believe anybody would watch *North of Sixty* if it didn't perpetuate stereotypes about Indians. There seems to be a need to view Indians as downtrodden and oppressed – it provides a reverse sense of superiority."

However, all the criticism of this show is tinged with a certain amount of understanding. Unfortunately, the vast majority of these issues do and are happening in Native communities all across the country. What irks me and a lot of other Native people is the refusal by the Powers That Be (specifically the producers and story editors) to show the other side of Native life – the humour and good times.

Throughout the horrific times, one of the things that has allowed us to face and overcome tragedies is our sense of humour. Read the works of most Native writers, and even in the deepest darkest moments of their characters' lives there is always a flash of humour. Amongst the Native community, this lack of realism seems to be the chief (no pun intended) complaint concerning *North of Sixty*.

When Native actress Columpa Bobb was asked to play the new nurse on the show, she vowed that the one thing that she would do was simply smile. Every time she entered a scene, she told herself to smile. "Nobody smiles on that show. I wanna be the first." And when her first episodes aired, she was indeed, the only one smiling. It looked obvious. Too obvious. She soon stopped. She said she looked like she was on drugs. But that's for a later episode no doubt.

According to a friend of mine who works on the show, the decision to not include humour in the life of the Native characters is deliberate and conscious. This friend also reports that anyone who criticizes the show becomes a *persona non grata* and will never work for the show again. So I shall refer to this peon as Deep Quiver.

My criticisms of the show are no secret to the Powers That Be. Deep Quiver tells me that for almost a year the following quote was scrawled across the top of the wall-sized blackboard in the room where they develop and plot stories for the show:

"North of Sixty is one of the most depressing shows on Canadian television and it does not accurately reflect Native life

– Drew Hayden Taylor"

I'm not sure if it was for inspiration or vengeance. The odd thing is, I don't remember ever actually saying that in any quotable environment. Up until now.

Deep Quiver has also told me that over the years the many members of the cast have quietly suggested that Native life is not entirely the way it's portrayed on the show – that Native people do laugh occasionally. But the Powers That Be respond that "its more dramatic" to focus on the problems.

Last spring I attended Dreamspeakers, an Aboriginal film festival in Edmonton. While there, I sat on a panel dealing with issues arising from *North of Sixty*. Also in attendance were several of the Powers That Be, the show's Cree/Metis story editor Jordan Wheeler, and story editor/producer Peter Lauterman. The floor was opened up to discussion and one of the first questions asked was, "If the show is about Native people, shouldn't it be more funny?"

Jordan Wheeler responded simply, "It's a drama. If you want comedy, watch a sit-com." He later told me he often gets asked the same question, even by the Dene of the N.W.T., the people whom the show is about. At the end of the panel, Peter Lauterman mumbled as he packed up his stuff, "If I have to explain why there's no humour one more time, I'll go crazy."

I don't buy Jordan's explanation. It's form over substance, with the form being the drama and the substance being Natives. Humour is so intrinsic to the culture, that to take the humour out of the characters to suit the form seems wrong. Some of the funniest moments I've ever seen have occurred in so-called drama, and some of the most emotional and touching scenes I've witnessed have happened in sit-coms.

Who knows? Maybe the Powers That Be will listen to their audience and lighten things up a bit. In these years of cultural renaissance, Native people want to celebrate who and what they are, not cry over it. Unfortunately, the show has a poor record of heeding its audience.

According to Deep Quiver, last season the show also introduced a character named Suzy Muskrat and the viewer response was larger than normal. Evidently the character touched many viewers and they wanted to see her back.

Instead, the Powers That Be shrugged it off theorizing it was just the actress organizing a letter-writing campaign to get more work.

After this, there's only one thing left to say. I'll probably never work in Lynx River again. I hope the *Toronto Star* is planning to put me in a Critic's Relocation Program.

ACADEMIA MANIA

Once upon a time, many years past, there was a man who told a story from his wayward youth. As he so bravely put it, it was a long time ago on a reserve far, far away, when he was but a young and innocent Aboriginal living with his family in the serene outdoors known today as Northern Ontario. Then one day, as often happens in tales such as this, a wandering group of archaeologists/anthropologists/sociologists (so grouped for they all looked and acted alike) appeared in his peaceful community.

It seems these intrepid academics were there in search of knowledge. They were fearless story-hunters, wanting to document the legends and myths of these proud but oral people. Legends they wanted, and legends they were determined to get, for the annals of history and their publishers. First in their quest they went to the Elders of the village saying, "Tell us your stories so that we may document them."

The Elders, believing stories are meant to be shared with good friends and caring people, refused, saying to the puzzled academics, "Strangers do not demand a story, they ask politely." Thus the academics were chastised. With no stories to bring back, and no victory to print, the academics pondered and prodded until they found willing confidants for their earnest, though ill-conceived purpose.

The children of that community boldly approached these White warriors of writing declaring, "We know the legends and stories of our people and we will gladly share them with you if you will honour us with gifts. Financial ones," spoke their young leader.

Eager and anxious, the academics gladly brought forth

their small change in trade for the fables and myths of these proud people. Every morning for many days, the children would entice these eager men with a legend of these proud forest people, often about the trickster Nanabush and his mischievous adventures, or about the animals that abound in this forest primeval, or occasionally about the people themselves.

And later, after the tale was told, the children of the community would retire to the woods from whence they sprang, and spend the afternoon enjoying the spoils of their barter. Down went the potato chips and pop they gladly consumed, all the while pondering and creating fresh new tales they would tell these pale strangers. For they kept close to their hearts the real stories of their people, and instead offered only the imagination and creativity of a child's mind. For what they traded were new legends, barely days old.

Many decades later, one of these children-turned-adult happened upon a book store. There, in a book of Native legends published many years before by a non-Native researcher, but used frequently as a source material, he came upon a story that was...oddly familiar.

Then it dawned upon him. In the pages he held in his hand were those same spirited stories commissioned all those years past. Childhood memories flooded his mind as he recalled those fun filled days of free junk food and gullible academics. "Ah," he thought, "the brilliant, mischievous days of youth." Seldom in his later years had he achieved such heights of roguish achievements.

The smile stayed upon his impish face as he replaced the book. The Trickster of legend was alive and well and living in the glorious halls of academia.

The Story Real: Some are tall, some aren't. Some are fat while others have a lean and hungry look about them. Most wear glasses or contacts, but not all. And believe it or not, some could be your next door neighbour. I am referring to academics.

There's an old joke in the Native community. What's the definition of a Native family? Two parents, a grandparent, five kids and an anthropologist (or academic). Get the picture?

Not a week goes by in the offices of the Native Earth Performing Arts, Toronto's only professional Native theatre company, that we don't get a call from some student or professor from a University/College doing research on Native theatre in Canada. And each time I put the phone down I struggle to suppress a shudder. I can't help but wonder – what wonderful images are they getting from our work?

When is a door not a door? When it's ajar. When is a symbolic metaphor describing the Native individual's relationship with the Earth, or Turtle Island as they call it, and the spiritual and physical sustenance that it provides, as well as the water being an allusion to the blood of said Turtle Island, or perhaps in this reference, the term Mother Earth would be more accurate, not a symbolic metaphor?

Sometimes you just wanna yell, "He's just fishing, for Christ's sake!"

This is a strange race of people who spend their entire life fulfilling some need to constantly study and analyse other people's writings and work (in this case Native works), but seldom attempt the same work themselves. It's sort of like people who watch pornographic movies but never have sex.

I remember reading an article written by British playwright Willy Russell, author of such plays as *Educating Rita* and *Shirley Valentine*. He was relating a story of a lecture he secretly attended; a lecture about his work.

At one point, the academic brought up for discussion the final scene of *Educating Rita*, where as a going-away gift, the former hairstylist Rita cuts the professor's hair. "This," said the man with letters behind his name, "was a direct metaphor to the Samson and Delilah legend where she is taking his strength by cutting his hair. The author obviously..."

At this moment, Willy Russell stood up and said, "Uh sorry, you're wrong. I just wanted to end the play on a funny and touching note. It has nothing to do with Samson." They proceeded to get into a rather intense argument over the interpretation of that scene. The academic refused to believe that Russell hadn't intended that final image to be a metaphor.

As a writer I recognize the fact that all stories, in whatever form they're written, are the equivalent of literary Rorschach tests, all open to interpretation and understanding. Often that's the fun of taking a literature class, dissecting the piece for the underlying imagery. And adding subtextual elements in the stories I write lends a certain amount of fun to the writing process.

However, as Freud used to say, sometimes a cigar is just a good smoke.

Case in point – a non-Native friend of mine wrote his master's thesis on Native theatre in Canada. In one of the chapters he examined some of my work. One night in a drunken celebration after successfully defending his thesis, he let me read his dissertation. As he celebrated his newfound academic status, I sat there reading some new and interesting theories about the symbolism in my plays.

To put it bluntly, they were wrong, completely way off, not correct, inaccurate, barking up the proverbial wrong tree. Especially the section where he thought a crow in the text was a manifestation of Nanabush, the Ojibway trickster figure. I sat there for a while, on that bar stool, quietly debating if I should tell him of the error.

But looking at the sheer joy in his face for all those years of university finally completed, I held my tongue. I'd rather have him drinking happily than in a fit of depression. If he thinks a crow is Nanabush, let him. There's a whole flock of Nanabushes living around my mother's house. He'd have a field day.

That seems to be the latest fad with academics. Subscribing all actions and at least one character in a written piece to the trickster figure. As playwright/poet Daniel

David Moses describes it, "They all like to play 'Spot The Trickster'."

But then again, these self-same people, the academics of this world, are responsible for introducing my books and other writings to the curriculum of various high schools, colleges and universities. The very computer I'm writing on I owe to their influences. So I guess I mustn't bite the hand that feeds me.

So perhaps, just for clarity's sake, I should take the time to make sure these no-doubt intelligent people understand that it's just the inherent trickster tendencies that exists on a subconscious level in all literary works penned by Aboriginal writers and are representative of our culture. In other worlds, I'm not responsible for these views or criticisms, the trickster is at fault here. The trickster made me do it.

Yeah, they'll buy that.

OUR HOME AND NATIVE CITY

I was visiting my mother on the reserve when it hit me. My own personal epiphany. I had been out for a country walk in the quiet evening air when I noticed something I hadn't seen since last year, and thus had forgotten. A single, tiny mosquito. And as is the mosquito mentality, within an incredibly short period of time, they were everywhere. And I do mean everywhere! Feeling like I was Pearl Harbour and the mosquitoes were Japanese Zeros, I had to do something. It was a good three quarters of a mile to my mother's house, but I made it faster than a promise out of Sheila Copps' mouth. There's an old Indian saying that answers the age-old question "How fast can you run?" "Depends what's chasing me."

As I scooted in through the door, barricaded behind an iron wall consisting of window screening (one of the best damn inventions by White people since air conditioning and Instabank machines), I noticed my mother and aunts laughing quietly. Their one statement revealed a sad but true reality.

"You've been in the city too long."

I have spent years denying it, ignoring the evidence, pretending it wasn't true, but I just can't do it anymore. I have reached a point of personal awareness in my life where I must face certain unavoidable realities, no matter how painful. After 16 years of living in Canada's largest city, I have finally admitted to myself that...I...am ...an...Urban Indian! There, I said it. It's time I came out of the metropolitan closet and acknowledged who I am.

Not that I have anything against Urban Indians. Some of my best friends are Urban Indians. But I just never thought I would ever be one. In just two more years I'll have spent exactly half my life in the big city, drinking cafe au laits, eating in Thai restaurants (it's hard to find good lemon grass soup on the reserve), riding the subways (also notoriously difficult to locate on the reserve), and having pizza delivered to my door, etc. I've grown soft.

A long time ago I heard an Elder wisely say to a group of young people. "We must go from being hunters in the forest to being hunters in the city." I now hunt for a good dry cleaners.

By trade I am a writer (though some might argue). I write plays, scripts, and short stories, oddly enough all taking place on an Indian reserve. In the past I used this simple fact to tell myself that though my body lived in an apartment near Bathurst and St. Clair, my spirit somehow was fishing in an unspoiled, unpolluted lake, nestled in the bosom of Mother Earth, somewhere up near Peterborough, Ontario.

Work and education were the reasons I originally came to Toronto those many years and pounds ago. I sought to explore the world outside the reserve boundaries and taste what the world had to offer. As with all things in life, there is a give and take involved in exploration. Instead of the easy, "I'll get there when I get there," saunter so many of my 'Rez' brothers and sisters have, I now have my own, "I have to get there in the next five minutes or life as I know it will end," hustle.

I've traded roving the back roads in pickup trucks for weaving in and out of traffic on my bicycle. Instead of blockading roads to defy authority, I refuse to wear a safety helmet. Where once I camped on deserted islands, I now get a thrill out of ordering room service in a hotel. Somehow it loses something in the translation.

Now, there are many people who live on reserves who feel you aren't a proper Native person unless you're born, live and die on that little piece of land put aside by the Government to contain Indians. How quickly they forget most Aboriginal nations were nomadic in nature. So when I tell these people "take a hike," I mean it in the most Aboriginal context.

I don't have to explain that I've spent eighteen years growing up in that rural community. It shaped who and what I am and if psychologists are correct, barring any serious religious conversion, I should roughly remain the same. The reserve is still deep within me. Given a few seconds of preparation, I can still remember the lyrics to most of Charley Pride's greatest hits. I can put away a good quart or two of tea. I can remember who the original six hockey teams were. And I know that contrary to popular belief, fried foods are actually good for you.

There is always the option, of course, that if the gods permit, I could return to the community that spawned me and reintegrate myself into the heart and soul of the reserve. That is most definitely an option, one that weighs heavily on my mind, and I think it's safe to say, on the minds of other Urban Dwellers of Aboriginal Descent (UDADs).

As my mother says, I know home will always be there. So will the mosquitoes and the gossip and relatives who still treat you like you are twelve years old...and those who walk in my moccasins know the rest.

Until then, if there is a then, I shall be content to acknowledge my current civic status. To celebrate, I think I shall go out this morning into this urban landscape, partake of some brunch and perhaps peruse a newspaper or two.

I may be an Urban Indian, but I'm also an Urbane Indian.

A View From a Café

Recently, I was sitting at an outdoor cafe enjoying some coffee and good conversation when I couldn't help noticing two men approaching the patio.

Still on the sidewalks, they came along the railing that enclosed the patio, stopping at each table, asking for money. They looked quite ragged, drunk, and had obviously seen better times. Both were Native. I am Native.

As I watched these two men of the street hustling money from a captive audience, I felt something. I wasn't sure what it was. Embarrassment, shame, pity? I had never felt these emotions toward fellow Natives before, and it troubled me.

As I sat there feeling ashamed, something occurred to me – what right do I have to feel ashamed of these men? It's their life, it's a free world. Then I began to feel ashamed of myself for taking such a high moral ground.

Over the past 13 years, I have been involved in various capacities with the media. During this time I have worked on approximately 17 documentaries about Native culture, arts and substance abuse. I have done enough research, been to enough communities, talked to enough of these people to know that in the vast majority of cases, it's not their fault that they live this existence.

I know all the stories and all the reasons.

Such factors as improper adoptions, the after-effects of residential schools, coming to the city seeking work and finding an environment totally alien and unwelcoming, despair over a disappearing culture, language and way of life – I could fill up the rest of this column with a steady stream of contributing factors. But the result would be the same. Tragic stories leading to a tragic existence.

But still, in the back of my mind, were these two men

pan-handling from middle-class White people, perpetuating stereotypes and giving credence to an image most Native people have spent their life fighting.

There was the case of one prominent Native artist in the city who, when approached for money, got into a terse discussion on the street with such a person, perhaps one of these very gentlemen, about the image they were presenting to the public. The discussion quickly deteriorated into an argument about attitude and rights and the artist walked away frustrated.

In this city, I have seen and constantly recognized approximately one to two dozen hard-core street dwellers in my daily travels who pursue the same practice as these two foraging men. On the other hand, there is an estimated Aboriginal population in Toronto of around 70,000 people. Not a bad ratio, all things considered.

But because of this preconceived alcohol-oriented luggage and the fact that visually, these Native people tend to stand out in one's memory more than say, a White street person, their image will stay with a passerby more readily.

I can see people at those patio tables saying when they get home, "A drunk Indian hit us up for money." And again I shudder.

Perhaps the fault is within myself. There is a term used in Ontario, most often Toronto, that is an offshoot of Anishnawbe – the word Ojibway people used to describe themselves and their people. Basically it translates as the 'original' or 'first' people.

The term has been modified to accommodate the growing Aboriginal middle-class that has appeared in Toronto and other major cities. They are sometimes referred to as 'Anish-snobs.'

I see these men, I know their story, I feel anger for what has happened to them, yet seeing them at the corner of Queen and Bathurst or at this patio, harassing people for money – against my will, I get embarrassed.

Does this make me a bad person?

FOR THE TIMES, THEY ARE A' CHANGIN'

3

Grey Owl is Dead, But His Spirit Lives On

Sometime during that ancient age known collectively as the sixties, there lived in the United States, a black activist and writer named Eldridge Cleaver. And during those tempestuous times this man noticed an unusual trend developing in the mating rituals of that period. It had become very apparent to him that more and more White women, specifically blondish types, seemed to be dating an awful lot of black men, and vice versa.

He chalked it up to these women wanting to rebel against the restrictive social norms of middle-class life, to upset their parents and the status quo of the day. This rebellious practice seemed to be in vogue back in those days. He also reasoned that the black men, wanting to sample the privileged world that had been denied to them by the dominant White society, thought this was great. Who were they to argue?

And because this new cross-cultural dating trend was first discussed in Cleaver's book *Soul On Ice*, it has been referred to, in some circles as the Soul-On-Ice Syndrome. The name says it all.

That was in the sixties. This is the nineties, and as they say, the more things change, the more they stay the same. Except this time, the trendy thing happens to involve Native people. Finding an Aboriginal companion seems to be all the rage these days. So, in the name of social commentary, I would like to rename the particular courting phenomenon – the Spirit-On-Ice Syndrome.

But in this case, we're not just talking about dating, we're talking about the whole enchilada (if I may appropriate that cultural metaphor). It seems that ever since *Dances with*

Wolves and *Dry Lips Oughta Move to Kapuskasing* hit the public, the White world is beating a path to the reserve door; seeking spiritual fulfillment, Elder's wisdom, and discount cigarettes.

Recently an Elder from my community told me about a visit by two White women to his house. These were the most recent in a regular influx of what he calls 'wannabe, groupies, and do-gooders' who, and I paraphrase their words, "I really-respect-and-honour-your-culture-and-want-to-be-a-part-of-it-so-please-let-me-participate-and-learn-from-your-sacred-and-ancient-ceremonies-so-I-can-understand-your-ways-this-isn't-just-a-phase-I'm-going-through-I-really-mean-it-so-can-I-huh?"

My Elder friend and I sat around for a good 45 minutes trying to figure out what, specifically, they wanted to 'understand?' Why we eat so much macaroni and tomatoes; why 75% of the Native population doesn't vote; and why we wear buckskin on hot summer days? (I haven't figured that one out yet myself.)

And this one blonde woman who was visiting my friend had recently divorced a black gentlemen. (I wonder if they met during the 60's?) Now she was becoming fascinated with Native culture and I guess Native men. At one point, according to her, her parents had asked her if she was ever going to date a White man, to which she replied, "I doubt it. They have no mystery."

Mystery? That was good for another 45 minute conversation with my Elder friend.

What mystery? We get up in the morning, put our clothes on, have coffee (usually fully or extra-caffinated), go to the bathroom... Yes, Indians do go to the bathroom but in a secret Indian way that can't be revealed. Maybe that's what she was talking about.

There are many more of these people than you would expect. A friend of mine went out last summer to attend a Sun Dance. When she arrived, she was one of the few Native people there. Eighty percent of the people setting up camp were non-Native. She was somewhat peeved.

There's also the story of this woman who went to Mexico, became enamoured with this Mexican Indian who took her into one of the Aztec ruins. There he told her about an ancient Aztec ceremony that involved making love on the steps of the pyramid. She believed and they did.

Stories like that remind me I'm only half an hour from the Peterborough Petroglyphs. Hmmm....

And there was this time I met this woman, quite casually, who was opening a Native art gallery. She introduced herself as being from the Six Nations Reserve in Southern Ontario. Several weeks later I asked her which of the Six Nations she was – Mohawk, Cayuga, etc. She looked at me for a moment then confessed that she was actually White, she had married into the reserve (she was now divorced), and she was quite proud of the fact that she still had her Status card.

Some weeks later she started dating an Alaskan Native painter, went to visit him, received an Indian name, and refused to be called by her own English name. She had her brand spanking new Indian name put on her business cards.

Is it any wonder my Elder friend and I are a little cynical? After 501 years of oppression, destruction, and general annoyance we are now, overnight, chic. Irony can be painful.

But I should be fair. Not all White people who come into our communities can be classified in this way. I have one aunt (who's French) who speaks better Ojibway than I do and has a thicker accent than me. And she didn't show up on our reserve all those years ago to 'understand.' She just fell in love and couldn't have cared less if my Uncle was Indian. Many other family members and friends fit into this category. They accept us as who we are, but they don't want to be us. Who can argue with that?

We also mustn't forget that there are some Native people out there that for one reason or another, want to be White. So we're willing to make you a deal. Ship ours back, and we'll ship yours back too.

WHAT'S IN AND WHAT'S OUT ON THE POW WOW TRAIL

In these increasingly confused times, one's grasp of what is proper and correct becomes more and more hazy. And like the dominant immigrant culture that surrounds them, Native people have fashion, social, and other trends that can change overnight. So if you're not careful, you can be caught practicing last years 'ins' creating a tremendous Indigenous faux pas that could alienate you from your friends for years. So I figure, White people have magazines and newspapers that tell them what's in and what's out. Why not Native people?

So now after years of extensive research listening to what's being said out there on the Pow wow trail, the bars, and McDonalds, I think I have come up with a preliminary list of what the in-tune Aboriginal is saying, doing, eating and thinking.

OUT	IN
Trying to be White	Trying to be Native
Telling stories and legends around the campfire.	Watching White people get rich and famous from writing stories, movies, novels, etc. about us
Residential school.	Therapy resulting from residential school
Hunting/gathering to survive	Treaty research
Tonto and the Lone Ranger (Hmmm, Kemosabe, what do we do now?)	*Dances with Wolves* (Hey Kev, what's next?)

OUT

Following the Pow wow trail
"I'm an Indian."

IN

Following the conference trail
"I'm a member of the
Aboriginal Native Indigenous
First Nations people.
(Actually, I'm Ojibway or
more accurately, Anishnawbe
Nation. Just call me Drew)

Wondering what happened to
all all the buffalo

Wondering what happened to
the funding

White liberals who want to
understand

White businessmen who want
to invest

Being asked, "What's it like
to be an Indian?"

Being asked, "Do you know
Graham Greene?"

Trapping (thanks to animal-
rights organizations)

Welfare (thanks to animal-
rights organizations)

Smoking cigarettes

Smuggling cigarettes

Grass (as in marijuana)

Grass (as in sweetgrass)

Indian men dating and
marrying blondes

Indian men sleeping with
blondes but marrying and
having children with Native
women

Being called before the court

Being called to the bar

W.P. Kinsella

Any speech by Ovide
Mercredi (unless it's over 20
minutes in length, then its
'out' and is replaced by any
thing from Tomson Highway)

Being cheated by land agents

Being cheated by court
sytems

OUT	IN
Native women saying "I'm a Feminist"	Native women saying "I'm Matriarchal"
Cowboys and Indians	Surete du Quebec and Warriors

Powwows, they are a' Changin'

When I was growing up, my mother used to talk about how much things had changed on the reserve from when she was a kid. I heard the countless stories of hauling innumerable pails of water from the pump, chopping wood, fighting swarms of Indian-loving mosquitoes without the protection of OFF, wading through armpit high snow to get to the outhouse as you battled hungry wolves, etc. You know, the usual stories.

But when you're young and stupid, you don't listen, let alone think of things having changed all that much. And as with the nature of the heavens, words like that eventually come back. I can't believe how much things have changed since I was a kid. Specifically, Pow wows.

Growing up on the Curve Lake First Nations Reserve in Central Ontario, I remember the social event of the season was our annual Pow wow held at (where else) the baseball diamond. While some of my cousins and other relations danced their buckskinned little hearts out, I'd run around on those hot dusty days, competing with all the other local kids to collect all the returnable pop bottles thrown away by the tourists. Hey, it was a living.

Now a days, everybody drinks from cans. Non-returnable cans. It's quite tragic when the end of an era is symbolized by an empty coke can being tossed into a garbage container.

Twenty years ago we used to think it was quite exotic when dancers from Akwesasne (a Mohawk community near Cornwall, Ontario) would come to dance at our Pow wow. We'd all stand around oohing and ahhing, pointing and whispering, "Wow. Look, real live Mohawks." I was at a Pow wow recently, where Native people from Central America, not to mention others from all over Canada and the United States, danced and sold things. People just a little more exotic then your average Mohawk to this now jaded eye.

In my day, the majority of dancers wore straight buckskin with the occasional colourful trappings attached. But if they were feeling adventurous and daring, it might be solid white buckskin.

In this day and age, the colours and designs of the dancers' regalia can dazzle your eyes and your pride. Fancy dancers, shawl dancers, grass dancers, jingle dress dancers, and traditional dancers (both male and female) have their own particular clothing style. You're lucky if you can find one in eight or nine dancers wearing a sizeable amount of buckskin. Fashion dictates have moved on.

The spectre of commercialism has also reared its head at today's Pow wow. At some of the larger gatherings, it's not uncommon to see tens of thousands of dollars of prize money being up for grabs. A few weeks ago I witnessed a group of tourists approach two young boys who were dressed in their dancing outfits. They marvelled over the boys for a moment then asked them if they could take their picture. Immediately both boys, in stereo, stuck up two fingers saying in well used practiced tones, "Two bucks." That's a long way from collecting pop bottles.

Food and craft booths have changed over the years. Eons ago, all the money I made on the pop bottles (after cashing them in) went directly back into the Pow wow through the purchase of God-awful amounts of traditional Native junk food like hamburgers, fried bread, corn soup and pop.

Today the list of traditional 'Native foods' being offered at Pow wows has grown to include pizza, candy floss, tacos, baloney on a scone, lemonade, etc. My favourite were these two stands side by side, one selling buffalo burgers (made from real buffalo), the other peddling something called an Indian burger (I can only hope it was made by real Indians, not from real Indians).

And I've given up trying to keep track of all the things for sale at these events. The gambit runs from your basic tacky tourist stuff to very expensive leather works, sculptures and paintings. Several dozen booths (some with inventive names like Imagin-Nations and Creative Native) hawk your standard Aboriginal paraphernalia like dream catchers, medicine wheels, glass beads, braids of sweetgrass, gobs and gobs of silver and turquoise etc.

Then there were the more. . .interesting things for sale. Playing cards designed in the style of your favourite Canadian tribe (I've got a full house, three Haida chiefs and two Cree medicine men – beat that!). Another booth was offering Tarot card readings, evidently a traditional Native activity I'm not familiar with. At one Pow wow I saw a booth selling a large selection of New Age books. One particular publication caught my eye – *How to be a Shaman In Ten Easy Steps*. Geez, all these years we've been doing it the hard way!

So, as I stood there in line waiting to use the portable Royal Bank Instabank conveniently located beside the port-a-pots, I couldn't help but marvel at all the changes over the years. Pow wows have gone high tech and modern. Then off in the distance I saw a man draining a bottle of pop (one of the large, still returnable sizes and then tossing it away. Feeling a twinge of nostalgia, I left the line, picked it up and put it in my bag. Some traditions never die.

DAVID AND MCGOLIATH: THE POLITICS OF FOOD

It was a beautiful Easter weekend and the Skydome was abuzz with the sounds of thousands upon thousands of people enjoying the first-ever Toronto International Pow wow. People of all nations were bustling around shopping at the Native arts and crafts booths, or watching the dancing and drumming taking place on the field. To these Pow wow jaded eyes, it looked like people were having a grand time.

I, on the other hand, was not. Off in the corner at one of the nine food booths that were to sell a variety of traditional Native cuisine, I was involved as a reluctant participant in an amazingly stupid corporate food fight. As strange as it may sound, it was between the clown and the deer.

Like all great wars, the inciting incident is often the silliest thing you can imagine. And far too often, innocent civilians are often drawn into the line of fire. Case in point: Native Earth Performing Arts, the Native theatre company I am affiliated with, had co-sponsored a Native nouvelle cuisine food stall with the award-winning and equally innocent Native chef David Wolfman. There we were, happily cooking away – grilling venison burgers, buffalo sausages, and heating a succulent salmon chowder, when the proverbial corporate boom was lowered.

According to a McDonald's spokesperson, who was making the first of several trips to our humble little stall, because of all the money the Big Mac Boys had put into the Skydome (which by the way is an Iroquois term used to describe the shape of the sky), we were not allowed to sell burgers or anything named a burger. If we did, they had full authorization and inclination to shut our little fundraising booth down. It seems the Quarter Pounder carries a lot of weight at the Skydome.

We had already been informed that we could not sell any soft drinks or coffee because of that same monopoly. Fine we thought, a little paranoid, but we figured if you're going to put millions into a place like this, you're entitled to some perks. But venison burgers? Somehow, I couldn't imagine David's tasty creations taking away any part of McDonald's market share. Somehow I had trouble imagining all those kids from Scarborough rushing out of the Towncentre McDonald's to get to the Skydome to buy a venison burger. David should be so lucky.

So not wanting to be argumentative, David changed the offending item to venison manwiches (though I had suggested the more PC name of Venison People-of-nonspecific gender wiches). Still not good enough according to the McPolice. It was still a meat patty in a bun. To the uninformed public, that would be a hamburger, or more specifically, a McDonald's hamburger. Uh huh.

David's bright solution – cut the burgers into quarters and sell them as grilled venison meatballs. It seems that was acceptable, except we were also informed that the meat had to be placed beside the bun, not inside the bun. Those damn hamburger bylaws again.

And to add further insult to bizarreness, our buffalo sausages seemed to the BMBs to resemble their hot dogs a wee too much so David was forced to cut them into one inch lengths to confuse the public. They also had to be put on the side, not in the bun. The hamburger bylaws, subsection B – the Hot Dog amendment.

Needless to say, we at the booth just shook our heads in amazement. One would think this enormous faceless entity would have better things to do than tell us we couldn't cook our traditional food.

Later that day my mother and I talked about the interesting events of the day. We marvelled at how well organized the Pow wow was overall, but we couldn't help but think how fortunate that it wasn't a dance or music studio that had put money into the Skydome, or all the dancers and drummers would have been out of luck, not to mention all the people who came to watch.

The we shook our heads over all the fuss being made about the buffalo and deer meat and its shape. She was pouring a cup of coffee from her thermos and I quickly told her to keep it hidden or the McPolice would get her. We had learned the fearful wrath of Ronald McDonald. Bambi had been run out of town.

A Native Perspective on Christmas

Well, it's here. That wonderfully perplexing season we all know and love as Christmas has arrived for yet another financially-draining year. And like every year, I tell myself, "Drew, don't get caught up in the whole buying, giving, getting, eating, burping, trying-to-find-my-jacket-after-the-last-Christmas-party mess."

I say this because I don't understand this whole yuletide thing. And no, I'm not going through a Scrooge phase. Actually I would call it more of a "let's try and rationalize the habits of White people and hopefully understand them" phase. As a Native person this is becoming more and more a full time job to me. I've been reading a lot of Desmond Morris lately.

Okay, let's start at the beginning. Christmas was created to celebrate the birth of Christ, right? Now doesn't that sound simple? But most historians agree Christ couldn't have been born on December 25th, but what the heck, let's celebrate anyway. Which in a way, turns out kinda okay. Luckily, all the Christmas carols take place in winter. *Dashing through the Snow* just wouldn't have the same effect in June. How about *Frosty the Mud Man* for May?

And try and find another historian who thinks it's possible that Christ was born in the year Zero. Uh uh. Most people think around 3 or 7 or 9 B.C. But let's start the first millennium off when he's in grade school. Go figure.

Let's look at it from another angle. When would it be the most inconvenient and difficult time of year to battle the elements and travel the icy roads to come home. How about the dead of winter? Oh, that makes a lot of sense.

Now traditionally, my people (the Ojibways) usually broke up into smaller family groups in the winter when it was harder to travel and there was less food to go around. This offered a better survival rate. Then they would merge back together in the summer when times were good and it made sense. But no, what did we know? We were backward savages. This coming from a race of people who, every year, wait in anticipation for some fat White man in a red suit, in a sleigh being pulled by flying reindeer, who travels the world pulling break and enters. And people leave cookies out for him. Now this is an advanced society.

And there's no use trying to combine the two different philosophies of winter life. People just get upset. An example: I had just arrived back in the city after spending a couple weeks at home for, you guessed it, Christmas, when I was invited to dinner with my roommate's relatives.

The evening was going along pleasantly enough when, curious about how Native people spent the holidays, they started to ask me what I did for Christmas. So I told them of a strange adventure I had experienced. I was walking home on Christmas Eve from visiting with friends when I noticed, in front of my house, a whole herd of large deer milling about something that looked like it had skis. The kids at the table started to get excited and asked me what I did then.

Well I told them I did what any self-respecting Indian would have done in that situation. I got my gun, shot them and ate them. We had several hearty Christmas meals, let me tell you.

I thought it was an interesting story, but for some reason it had upset my roommate's family, especially the kids. So trying to apologize and get back in the family's good graces, I held up my duffel bag and said, "I have some steaks left over. They're in here. Want some?" Again I said something wrong.

Now any self-respecting Native family would have jumped

at the chance for fresh venison, especially these ones. They had such a . . . light taste to them. Not heavy like some meat. Not like the rabbit I caught last Easter.

ABORIGINAL LOVE IN THE '90s

Being Native in this whacked-out country called Canada can be difficult at the best of times, and at the worst of times. . .well, let's just say these days Oka stands for more than a particular brand of cheese (which it does, by the way).

On top of the regular daily burdens of Aboriginal life in Canada, being a single Native person in today's society only adds to the difficulty. Traditionally, in bygone days, there were tried and true practices for getting single, eligible people together to marry and make little moccasin wearers. Unfortunately, like so many other traditions, these have gone the way of competency in government.

So what does a young (or not so young) Native person do when his heart turns to the idea of love and where to find it? I know of far too many single Natives wondering where all the good 'skins are hiding and how to find them. Well, there are several options available to the lonely Indian. He/she could follow a number of conferences or sports tournaments that have become the select meeting ground for upwardly and laterally mobile Native people.

Basically, these conferences and tournaments are the Aboriginal equivalent of a singles bar. There's also the old stand-by for the more tradition-minded – the Pow wow trail – where the concept and practice of 'snagging' has become a fine art.

In fact, unless you know the ground rules or proper terminology, the action gets confusing. A non-Native friend and I were working on a project with some other Native people when she, quite innocently, asked loudly across the room if she could 'snag' me for a few moments. All eyes turned to the two of us and I remember the perplexed look on her face, and the anticipation on mine. That was, of course, until she learned the Aboriginal connotations of that word, and well. . .

Several theories have been put forward concerning why meeting people is so hard these days. One school of thought blames it on the romantic literature that has been forced upon us instead of our traditional stories. Take *Romeo and Juliet*, two star-crossed lovers whose parents are at war. In desperation, the lovers end up committing suicide together. A great tale by a great writer, I'll admit.

What wonderful piece of literature are we presented with? Remember the song *Running Bear*, about two star-crossed lovers whose tribes are at war, and they end up committing suicide in the middle of a river? It was written by someone known as the Big Bopper. Now, what's wrong with this picture?

And to the best of my knowledge, I have yet to come across any self-respecting Aboriginal person who knows anything vaguely resembling the famous 'Indian Love Call.' I personally tried the Jeannette McDonald version in a few Indian bars. You know, "When I'm calling you. . .ooouuu. . .oouu. . ." It doesn't work. Trust me.

The few dates I have had lately can loosely be categorized into what I call the three 'tics.' They are sometimes erotic, possibly exotic, and unfortunately, usually neurotic. That's why I wasn't surprised when my doctor told me I didn't have a heart anymore. Just scar tissue.

But Native people are adaptable – the climate changes, so they change with the climate. And typically, it starts off with Native women taking the bull by the horns, so to speak. A while ago, several single Native women I know were lamenting about being single, and that there seemed to be so many of them floating around out there with no direction. Since there is power in numbers, they decided to band together to form a Native womens' singles organization.

What to call themselves was first on the agenda. Several

names were bandied about, but the one that seemed to catch their imagination was a slightly modified version from the movie *Steel Magnolias*. Since Native women don't have a 'steely' colour, and have instead that wonderful brown shading, they decided to call themselves. . .the Copper Magnolias.

But as it was quickly pointed out, what is a good single Native womens' organization without a single Native mens' organization? That's how I got drawn into this. I was approached to found and name the male equivalent of their organization, for social events, etc. My brain toiled with the challenge. There was obviously no shortage of membership, so that was taken care of. But what to call our beloved association? I had to come up with a name that we would be proud to call ourselves. A name that would fully describe the experience of the single Native male. Then it came to me. Our name and symbol would be. . .the Standing Pine Club.

As I write this, chapters of both organizations are being formed all across the country. Except in the Arctic, where there are no Standing Pines, only Standing Lichens. Somehow it doesn't have the same impact.

Aboriginal T.V.

It came upon me before I knew what hit me. I'm talking about Fall. It has arrived yet again signalling another well-publicized colourful extravaganza of seasonal battles. No, I am not talking about the beauty of the changing leaves or the wrapping up of numerous sports seasons. No, I talk once again of being thrust into another war amongst the airwaves. The new television season has arrived.

New shows, new stars, but oddly enough many of the new shows have the same feel as shows gone by. Could it possibly be that these shows have perhaps, just maybe, the same premise as earlier shows? You know what they say, 'there is nothing new under the sun'. Or is there?

With talk rampant amongst the Federal, Provincial and Aboriginal governments concerning the implementation of some form of self government by 1998, anything could be possible. Picture it in your mind, if you dare, the fall of that pivotal year. You tune in on your brand new 3-D television to watch the brand spanking new season of the Aboriginal Broadcasting Network. There's a big bowl of popcorn on your lap, a bowl of corn soup on the table, in your hand a bottle of diet pop because your favourite chair now makes a noise when you sit down in it. Then you press the "on" button to tune in.

"All in the Clan" The comic everyday lives of a family embroiled in the fast changing world of their reserve as different generations often bump heads over important social issues.

Nah, too silly, viewers would be expecting White people in sheets or something. You flip the channel.

"Akwesasne Vice" The adventures of two undercover special constables as they struggle to stem the flow of illegal cigarettes flooding over the Canadian/U.S. border.

Nah, too violent. Besides it's hard to make a pick up truck and plaid lumber jacket look sexy. You flip the channel.

"Curve Lake K0L1R0" How about the tale of a family with good looking, if annoying, teenagers moving from up north to a rather prosperous and up-scale Indian reserve located in Southern Ontario?

Oh please, if I want to hear whining or people upset, I'll tune in a constitutional conference or a First Minister's meeting. There's always one somewhere.

"Longhouse on the Prairies" Stay tuned for the touching, heartwarming story of an Iroquois family moving out to the Canadian midwest to start a new life as farmers. Or how about the Inuit version, "Little Igloo On The Tundra?"

Oh please, I'm borderline diabetic as it is. This would push me over the edge. Flip the channel again.

"Cree's Company" The fun continues as we join the wacky and comic adventures of a small overcrowded reserve. Jack is introduced to two beautiful women who have just recently been reinstated. Due to the lack of adequate housing, they are forced to live together in his small cramped house.

Evidence of a once proud civilization. I wonder if we can blame this on Columbus, too? Flip.

"Maritime Residential School" Immediately followed by the misadventures of five wildly different teenage girls as they laugh, love and learn to get along with each other while living together at the Maritime Residential School. Stay tuned for "The Micmacs Of Life."

I could be out mowing my grass right now, or raking the leaves, getting a heart attack and dying. Tough decision. Flip.

"Shacked up with Kids" And for the Native community's most dysfunctional family, Al, Peg, Kelly, and Bud Benojee, don't miss "Shacked Up With Kids." This is actually closer to life than you'd think.

No wonder people always told stories around the campfire, if the storyteller told a bad story, you could always set them on fire. Think about it people.

What's an Expert To Do?

What do you do when, through no fault or intention of your own, practically everybody considers you an expert? And you aren't, but nobody listens to that. If you decline this flattering but inaccurate assessment, people think one of two things:

1. You're just being modest. Which seems to make things even worse because it makes them want your opinion even more; or

2. They conclude you're ducking the question, or favour or work that requires your supposed expertise, thus pissing them off.

In truth, I am a writer who knows a few things about how to write a play, a television script, literacy, journalism, and how to lose at poker badly. If you throw in scads and scads of useless trivia about television and movies, and everyday Native life, you have about the extent of my knowledge. Not that impressive is it?

But for some reason, there's a train of thought out there in the mainstream world we call Society that states that anybody who gets things published can answer practically any question about anything. Now, make that writer a Native person, regardless of background, and he is supposed to have an encyclopedic knowledge of issues, customs, cultures and personal family names of every Native person from the Pacific to the Atlantic and up to the Arctic.

It is not uncommon for me, for example, to be asked by a non-Native person if I know a Native person from Alberta that he met at a conference. I ask if they could be a tad more specific and they respond with, "Well, I think he was Cree." That certainly narrows it down. "His last name might have been Cardinal." Well, in the Alberta Cree community that's like saying his first name is John. I end up having to apologize for not knowing this individual immediately. There are still a few hundred thousand Native people in this country I haven't gotten around to meeting yet.

Another example of my presumed all-around proficiency is the number of cassettes and CD's that have poured into my office from Native musicians. Evidently they think I can, in some capacity, review them. I can't, but they make great paper weights. Several weeks ago I received a request from a Native magazine to review Don Ross's new CD. Don is a phenomenal Micmac classical guitarist. But I had to point out that my knowledge of music is somewhat limited to anything I already know the words to. It also doesn't help that I don't own a CD player.

Just recently I received a call from a producer interested in turning a short story with a tenuous Native-connection in it, into a half hour drama for television. As part of the process he wanted me to read the piece and come up with some comments about the correctness or authenticity of the spiritual elements of the story. There are many things in life I am: an Elder or medicine person I am not. Like many people my age and my profession, I have a certain level of understanding concerning spiritual matters, but I am by no means an expert.

But these people don't care. I'm Native, that's all that matters to them It's all supposed to be in my blood (evidently my Native corpuscles have overcome the Caucasian part of my haemoglobin). What's a guy to do?

By sheer exposure, though, you do learn to expect a certain amount of inquisitiveness. I don't think there's been a week in the last three and a half years that I haven't been asked somewhere by somebody, my personal opinion (from an Aboriginal perspective, of course) about either Oka or *Dances With Wolves*. For the record, I thought both had some high drama, a few tears, some laughs, people learned some things about Native people, and I especially liked the fact the Indians were the good guys and the army were the bad guys.

And both were left ripe for sequels. I bet the same guy wrote both scripts.

But perhaps the most telling area for an 'expert' is the complex world of politics. During the wild and wacky months we called Meech Lake, every time I went home I was asked to explain, as simplistically as possible, what the hell was going on? What was all the fuss about?

Unfortunately my knowledge of politics is often limited to watching, or sometimes participating in, what goes on at family gatherings or in bars. So in order to fake it, I make things up about the White government's need to make things more complicated than they need to be. But the fact is I think I was closer to the truth than I intended.

During the last election I was asked several times to write a political commentary on the issues and candidates. It's amazing what you can fake when people wave a cheque in front of your face. I really must get around to finding out who won that election.

That's my dilemma. You fess up and tell these people you're not qualified and they tell you to just offer an opinion or write something anyway – they're sure it will be wonderful. I have toyed with the idea of going back to school to find some sort of academic base to respond to these questions, but I wouldn't know where to start, due to the wide variety of subject matter I get asked about. I might end up in school for eons and eons and by the time I got out, I'd be a boring academic whose opinion nobody wanted.

So when all's said and done, I guess I'm left seeking comfort in the words of Vladimir Nabokov who once said, "I am sufficiently proud of my knowing something to be modest about my not knowing everything."

Okay, so I know a few things.

WHAT'S GOOD FOR THE GOOSE

The Referen-dumb is done and finished. Thankfully this particular nail biter has bitten its last nail. For now at least.

Decisions have been made, careers won and lost, an old country saved and a new country prevented. But in this land still called Canada, one that prides itself on being a law-abiding, government-conscious nation, there is one question left to be answered: When are Lucien Bouchard and Jacques Parizeau going to be tried for treason?   Don't get me wrong. I personally am not calling for Bouchard and Parizeau to be hung from the neck until dead as historical tradition dictates. I'm sure they're both wonderful and truly dedicated people, though as a person of Native ancestry I belong to one of those troublesome 'ethnic groups' the separatists have a problem with. Unlike some people living in Canada, part of me admires them for their tenacity and dedication. But my point of issue here is that it sure would be nice to have a sense of continuity or of equal justice in these difficult times.

I am, of course, referring to the year 1885 when, on the orders of Prime Minister John A. Macdonald himself, Louis Riel was tried, convicted and finally hung for the crime of treason – treason being defined as "a violation of the allegiance owed to one's sovereign or state; betrayal of one's country."

As any student of Canadian history is aware, Riel's crime of treason was his struggle to band together the Metis and various Native nations of the west into an independent state, defiant and autonomous of the Canadian government. And again as most Canadians are aware, they failed after a valiant attempt.

And since the British system of law (like many others) has

a very low tolerance for treason, Mr. Riel was strung up for daring to envision a separation from Canada. For having the dream of setting up an independent country along the lines of a distinct culture, language and land base. Does any of this sound familiar?

Little did he realize all of this would come into vogue a mere century or so after his hopes and life were ended. Perhaps Riel was just ahead of his time. Now-a-days, instead of engaging in bush battles and fleeing from government forces to the States, he'd be elected head of the Opposition in the House of Commons. And instead of holding Referendums, he'd be using such age-old Aboriginal tricks as blockading roads like, say, the 401. What would Sir John A. Macdonald have to say about that, I wonder?

Now all this begs the question, why was Louis Riel hung as a traitor while Bouchard collects an impressive salary? There are many similarities between the two – both have French ancestry, both have an American connection, both have cultures they were struggling to preserve. Yet Riel lies in his grave, a disgrace to some, a hero to others, while Bouchard may get promoted up the political ladder as a hero (and I suppose, a disgrace to some).

A cynic might say it was because Riel was Metis and Bouchard is French. A historian may believe times have changed even though the wish to separate from Canada hasn't. Me? I just blame it on Canadian politics. I long ago gave up expecting reason and logic when it comes to running this country.

So here we are. Two people who have tried to do the same thing. Both failed, receiving two different reactions to their efforts.

If I am to understand that history repeats itself, but winners and losers change with the wind, anything and everything is possible. Who knows, maybe the politics of Brian Mulroney will live again. Hey, platform shoes made a comeback, for some godforsaken reason.

And as for Lucien, a word of advice. Politics and times change. I'd stop wearing those neckties so tight if I were you.

Is Good for the French Gander

To anybody following the on-going political soap opera currently running in Ottawa and Quebec, it almost seems that God does have a sense of humour, or at the very least, a sense of irony. I am, of course, talking about the sudden spate of threats concerning the potential partition of a possibly independent Quebec into smaller, culturally specific fiefdoms.

It's such a ludicrous change of events, a twist of fate per se that can only be properly explained by the use of exceedingly bad cliches. Evidently turnabout *is* fair play.

Now that the proverbial tables are turned, Quebec is saying, "You can't do that. We can, but you can't!" I guess it's a simple case of do what I say, not what I do. With still lingering memories of incidents like Oka and the bizarre comments from the P.Q. leaders about those pesky 'ethnic voters,' and the birth rate of White people in the province, it's no wonder the Inuit and Crees of Northern Quebec want to pick up their toys and go back home to Canada, should the province separate. It's a matter of choosing the lesser of two evils.

Now that the shoe is on the other foot, I can't help but wonder if it won't be too long before we start seeing television commercials flooding the Quebec airwaves with such slogans as, "My Quebec includes the Ungava Peninsula" or "My Quebec includes the Gatineaus." Provincial unity rallies will be held all across La Belle Province. I see bus loads of Parti Québécois supporters making forays into the nether regions of the province, showing up in isolated Aboriginal communities saying with a smile, "It just won't be the same Quebec without you guys." It's possible.

But if this is their bed and they have to lie in it, then they should be happy. For if all these regions of questionable P.Q.

loyalty were to exit the political entity of Quebec, that would leave a couple hundred square miles of pure French territory. After all these years of being the oppressed minority, they will be able to proudly rule as a majority along both banks of the St. Lawrence. While they may lose in quantity, they will no doubt revel in quality.

If it is simply a case of dishing out but not being able to take it, the Quebec government should be aware that if you live in a glass house, you shouldn't throw political stones. They just might boomerang.

As for the Native people of the province, it is not just a case of wanting back the land that the province says they surrendered to the government long ago. That, of course, would make them Indian givers. It's simply a matter of wanting to maintain their cultural and linguistic individuality in an environment dominated by another forceful and aggressive society. Sound familiar?

But no sense in the pot calling the kettle black. Another reference to those irksome 'ethnic voters' again? Oh well, it takes one to know one.

ABORIGINAL LEXICON

Linguistic terms often used in relation to Canada's Indigenous people are fast becoming words of everyday use. But sometimes these words have a specific and contextual meaning, above and beyond their accepted use. To help cut down on potential misuse and misunderstandings, I have put together a list of contemporary Aboriginal buzz words to help facilitate the proper dialogue. Please use them with care.

Assembly of First Nations:
Political organization claiming to represent all Status and Reserve Natives except for those who have opted out, like the Iroquois Confederacy and certain Western tribes. Sort of like the situation in the former Soviet Union.

Blockades:
Pre-ordained trump card, or why else would the Creator have placed a large portion of necessary and needed roads on Native territory.

Dreamcatchers:
Aboriginal merchandising at its best. They are everywhere.

Government (1):
Source of all evil.

Government (2):
Source of all funding, allowing various Native organizations to criticize government (1).

Indian Giver:

A case of saying one thing but reversing it and doing the opposite. Like treaties.

Kashtin:
Simon and Garfunkel with a tan.

W.P. Kinsella:
Aboriginal enemy #1, or the second coming of Shakespeare if you have anything to do with the new television series based on *Dance Me Outside* called *The Rez*.

Land Claims:
Native equivalent of Karma.

Minister of the Department of Indian Affairs:
Person who has no real grasp of what's going on out there but acts like he does. Like the U.N.

Native/Quebec Relations:
An oxymoron.

Oka:
Where past treatment meets current reality. See Malcolm X's comment concerning the assassination of JFK, "A case of the chickens coming home to roost."

Pocahontas:
In film, Tonto in drag, or in reality, a 12-year-old with a fabulous publicist.

Quebec:
Province wanting sovereignty from Canada but unwilling to allow Native communities the same right within Quebec. A case of "do as I say, not as I do."

Self-Government:
Self determination or the right to have our own Trudeau or Mulroney.

Tobacco:
Sacred ceremonial herb or cursed addictive plant, depending on how long your family has been in this country.

Treaty Rights:
Not to be confused with hunters & anglers, logging, mining or government wrongs.

Wannabe:
Elements of mainstream society suffering from culture-envy. The Anti-apple.

White People:
Politically incorrect term for those of European descent. More currently acceptable terms are People of Pallor, Colour-Challenged, or the Pigment-denied.

Wine/Beer/Liquor:
Tasty recreational beverages or cursed addictive intoxicant, depending on how long your family has been in this country.

Defining a philosophy of life can be a complicated matter. Sometimes too complicated. After several years in the Canadian school system, it became only too evident how the philosophies of life can be made more complex than they really are.

I know Europeans have spent untold eons thinking about how they think. Well, that's fine and dandy if you have nothing else to postulate about. But on the reserve, the philosophies of life are much simpler. And you don't need a Ph.D. to understand them either. All you need is common sense.

- Never trap on another person's trap line.
- Enjoy the variety of life, that's why the Creator made four seasons.
- When something goes wrong, you can usually blame a politician.
- Family will be there when strangers won't.
- Animals are often brighter than people.
- Beware of unusually coloured snow.
- Never kill more than you can eat.
- Life is a circle, try not to get lost.
- It's easier to go with the current than against it.
- Be sure and read the fine print.
- When the government promises something, make sure there's a camera crew there.
- Whenever you hunt an animal, make sure it's not hunting you.
- The real difference between Whites and Natives is: White people have a square dance, Native people have a round dance.
- Who needs money when you've got a horse (or buffalo)?
- Be careful who you date, they could be your relation.
- Eat drink and be merry for tomorrow they may put you on a reserve.
- Nobody can see tomorrow with out first looking at yesterday.
- Lead an interesting life and somebody will make a movie about it.
- Be careful where you point your arrows, they might actually

strike.

•Check the authentic Native totem pole for a 'Made in Korea' label.

•God works in mysterious ways and White people work in strange ways. When all else fails, threaten to put a land claim on them. Everything in the universe is connected, are you?

ACKNOWLEDGEMEMTS

The essays in this collection were previously published as follows:

Pretty Like A White Boy	*This Magazine*
An Ojibway in Mohawk Territory	*Windspeaker*
Summer of Our Discontent Revisited	CBC Radio
The New Two Solitudes	*Kahtou*
Ich Bin ein Ojibway	*This Magazine*
Paradise Lost	CBC Radio
Why the Butt Stops Here	*Windspeaker*
The Fish/Indian Wars	*Windspeaker*
Missionary Positions & Vegetarian Warriors	*This Magazine*
The First Nail in DIAND's Coffin	*Windspeaker*
An Aboriginal Name Claim	*The Globe & Mail*
An Indian by any other Name	*The Globe & Mail*
What Colour is a Rose?	*The Toronto Star*
Call of the Weird	*The Toronto Star*
Coloured Movies: Aboriginals on Parade	*The Toronto Star*
Pocahontas: Beauty and the Belief	*The Toronto Star*
Waiting For Kinsella	*The Toronto Star*
Whatever Happened to Billy Jack	*The Globe & Mail*
What Natives Were Talking About in 1993	*The Globe & Mail*
North of Sixty, South of Accurate	*The Toronto Star*
Academia Mania	*The Toronto Star*
Our Home and Native City	*This Magazine*
A View From a Cafe	*The Toronto Star*
Grey Owl Is Dead, But His Spirit Lives On	*The Globe & Mail*
What's In & What's Out on the Pow wow Trail	*The Globe & Mail*
Powwows, they are a' Changin'	*The Globe & Mail*
David and McGoliath: The Politics of Food	*Windspeaker*